Reference Skills for the School Librarian

Reference Skills for the School Librarian: Tools and Tips

Third Edition

Ann Marlow Riedling,
Loretta Shake, and
Cynthia Houston

 LINWORTH

AN IMPRINT OF ABC-CLIO, LLC
Santa Barbara, California • Denver, Colorado • Oxford, England

Library of Congress Cataloging-in-Publication Data

Riedling, Ann Marlow, 1952–
   [Reference skills for the school library media specialist]
   Reference skills for the school librarian : tools and tips / Ann Marlow Riedling, Loretta Shake, and Cynthia Houston. — Third edition.
      pages cm
   Includes bibliographical references and index.
   ISBN 978-1-58683-528-6 (paperback) — ISBN 978-1-58683-529-3 (ebook)
   1. School libraries—Reference services—United States. 2. Children's reference books. 3. Children's electronic reference sources. 4. Internet in school libraries. I. Shake, Loretta. II. Houston, Cynthia. III. Title.
   Z675.S3R54 2013
   025.5'2778—dc23   2012036617

ISBN: 978-1-58683-528-6
EISBN: 978-1-58683-529-3

17 16 15 14 13   1 2 3 4 5

This book is also available on the World Wide Web as an eBook.
Visit www.abc-clio.com for details.

Linworth
An Imprint of ABC-CLIO, LLC

ABC-CLIO, LLC
130 Cremona Drive, P.O. Box 1911
Santa Barbara, California 93116-1911

This book is printed on acid-free paper ∞
Manufactured in the United States of America

Contents

PART 1

What is Reference All About?

Chapter 1

Reference and the School Library: An Overview

Introduction

It is said that there exists a university library in the United States that has carved over its front entrance, "The half of knowledge is knowing where to find it." I would like to add the following words: evaluate, organize, and use of information. School library media reference services, in the past, as now, assist students to get a better value from the library media collection than they would have on their own. Reference for school librarians is more than a skilled technique. It is a profoundly human activity ministering to one of the most basic needs of humans, the desire to know. Reference processes, sources, and services revolve around the basic principle of maximization of resources, which underlies all reference work.

It is human nature to be curious. Throughout our lives, we seek answers to all kinds of questions. Having a healthy curiosity and a willingness to seek answers is a prerequisite for lifelong learning. In our electronic information age there appears to be more answers than questions, and our greatest difficulties with information lie in finding the most authoritative answer using the best sources possible.

Information Inquiry and Reference Services

As the saying goes, "Inquiring minds want to know." A 21st-century update for this saying would be, "Inquiring minds want to know the correct information quickly." The growing number of applications on the Web that are linked to mobile devices helps us find answers to our daily questions anywhere and anytime. However, to be able to determine what information best fits our needs at any point in time involves a skill called "information literacy" and a process called "information inquiry." It all begins with an information problem, based on a question, problem to solve, or just plain curiosity.

Based on the information problem, a plan to locate possible answers is developed using evaluative reading and information skills, in order to understand various kinds of information in different media formats. When the plan is executed, the result is a synthesis of information that is then applied to the problem. Sometimes, the information problem is as simple as locating the correct date for a particular event. Other times the problem is more complex. Regardless of how simple or complex the information problem, the overriding goal of the information inquiry process is to answer a question, solve a problem, or communicate information to a particular audience.

In the school setting, although curriculum changes occur often, students' need for information will always exist. While student dependence upon the Internet to find the answers to their questions has increased, the school librarian's role as provider of quality information resources and as a guide for using information resources effectively will always be important. What the school librarian does with regard to reference services is fundamentally to assist students in finding the answers to questions and helping them become independent users of information and ideas. To fulfill this role, the school librarian must have the ability to translate student questions into terms that can be understood by aligning them with proper resources. This is known as *reference services*. As explained by Kenneth Whittaker, "The purpose of reference and information service is to align information to flow efficiently from information sources to those who need it. Without the [school librarian] bringing source and [student] together, the flow would either never take place at all or only take place inefficiently" (1977, 49). In essence, the school librarian acts as a mediator between the perplexed student and too much, or too little, information. As a mediator, the school librarian weighs the good, the bad, and the indifferent data to locate accurate sources to meet the information needs of students and to assist students in determining what they need out of the ever-growing masses of print and electronic information.

There has been quite a lot of research done over the years on students and information skills instruction, some of which tie media center and information literacy instruction directly to student achievement. A comprehensive review of research done on school libraries and achievement indicates that there is a significant relationship between the quality of information services provided in the media center and student learning demonstrated on state and national achievement tests. Results of these studies indicated that there is a significant positive relationship between the quality of reference sources and services provided in the school and student learning and that effective school library programs provide a broad range of reference materials. A number of state studies indicate that when students receive regular instruction in information literacy, when information literacy is an integrated part of the school curriculum, and when information literacy is taught in collaboration with teachers, student achievement increases (Scholastic, 2008).

Because student achievement is linked with the library programs promoting effective use of reference and information services, it is essential that school librarians understand its key features. Successful reference services for school librarians consist of three components: 1) knowledge of the library media collection, electronic information resources, and tools; 2) effective conversational skills (communication); and 3) competence in selecting, acquiring, and evaluating resources to meet students' needs. Corresponding with these three components are two basic functions of library media center services: 1) the provision of information and 2) instruction or guidance in the use of information sources. The American Library Association explains that school libraries exist for the purpose of information and enlightenment. They are institutions with an educational [instruction] and informational [provision of information] purpose.

The accurate and appropriate provision of information will occur when the school librarian has a complete and accurate knowledge of the library collection, along with competence in selecting, acquiring, and evaluating that collection. School library collections consist of a variety of resources; what is a resource? A resource is any source or material, regardless of form or location, that provides necessary answer(s). According to AASL's *Empowering Learners* (2009) the library media program should provide, "a well-developed collection of books, periodicals, and non-print materials in a variety of formats that support curricular topics and are suited to inquiry learning and the user's needs and interests" (38). (Proper selection and evaluation processes and techniques are discussed in the following chapter.)

Instruction or guidance in the use of information sources by the school librarian is dependent upon effective conversational (communication) skills. It has been suggested that the school is an agency of communication, with constant interactions between librarians, teachers, students, and information. Because of all these communication exchanges, providing guidance is vitally important. The school librarian should never lose sight of the fact that, to the student, the question is only partly a technical requirement; at a deeper level that information is required to satisfy a basic cognitive need. (Effective communication and conversational skills and techniques are addressed in more detail in chapter nine.)

Instruction or guidance reference services teach or direct students to locate information themselves. It provides them with an understanding of reference tools and techniques, their correct usage, and how the school library and information resources are organized. Instructional services also advise and assist students in the identification and selection of appropriate materials about a given topic. Instruction or guidance may occur with individuals or groups; however, the end result remains the same—educating students regarding access, evaluation, organization, and use of reference sources. It is important to remain aware of the fact that school librarians lead students to information (many times on their own), not knowledge. Students manipulate the information and construct knowledge from that information.

School librarians often provide orientations to inform students as to the organization and scope of the school library's resources. This is a significant aspect of reference services for school librarians. Additionally, orientations are many times employed as a means of welcoming students and encouraging visitation to the school library.

Reference instruction is also termed *bibliographic instruction*. Bibliographic instruction is an expression widely used and accepted in the modern library world. It is defined as any activity that is designed to teach students how to locate and use information in the library, as well as sources that exist beyond the physical boundaries of the school library. Reference instruction can be as straightforward as assisting students with a quick question or "ready reference" by helping them to understand how to use online search engines to find authoritative answers to simple questions. On the other hand, reference instruction could also be as complex as guiding students through the use of a number of different reference sources and the information inquiry process as part of a research assignment. With the explosion of technologies that exist within and beyond the walls of library media centers today, the term *bibliographic instruction* more accurately defines what school librarians do with regard to reference work and the education of today's students—teaching lifelong learning skills. This fact is emphasized in the AASL's *Empowering Learners* (2009), which states that the library media program "models an inquiry-based approach to learning and the information search process" (19).

The Reference Process

Based on the previous discussion, we can easily see that the day of seeking answers has not ended; only the process has changed. What is the reference process? Fundamentally, it consists of the entire transaction with the student in the course of which the reference work is carried out. Basically, it contains three primary elements: 1) information; 2) student; and 3) answer. These elements combine with five specific steps to create the complete reference process: 1) a need for information; 2) a question; 3) the search for information; 4) an answer or response; and 5) an evaluation. (Figure 1.1 more thoroughly

---

Figure 1.1: The Reference Process: Five Basic Steps

1. A Need for Information
   A request is made.
2. A Question
   What problem needs solving? What decision or choice needs making?
   What data and insight are required to shed light on the main question?
   What are the smaller questions that will help create an answer to the primary question?
   What does the student already know? What is missing?
   What does the student not know?
3. The Search for Information
   Based on the question(s), the student and school librarian develop research problem-solving strategies.
   Where might the best information lie?
   What sources are likely to provide the most insight with the most efficiency?
   Which resources are reliable?
   What steps will be required to protect against bias and develop a balanced view?
   Which sources are the most current?
   Location and identification of resources occurs.
4. An Answer or Response
   Information is sorted and organized; synthesis should occur.
   Are different resources required? Are additional resources required?
   Is the information provided complete?
   Does the student understand the information?
   Is the student information literate? Has the student learned how to learn?
5. An Evaluation
   Has the need(s) been met?
   Was the reference process complete or incomplete?

---

explains these five steps in the reference process.) The reference process may be simply explained as problem solving. It is the solution of the student's problem that is the real object of the process. As fixed as this process may appear, school librarians must keep in mind that each question is unique; therefore, each process will be unique as well. The reference process is merely an outline; what occurs within the text differs from situation to situation, student to student.

Reference, Information Literacy, and Information Inquiry

In the technological, global society of today, information literacy, defined as the effective use of information sources in all formats, cannot be overlooked. The essential philosophy surrounding school library reference service is the encouragement of lifelong learning, or information literacy. The American Library Association (2006) describes information-literate individuals as "those who have learned how to learn. They know how to learn because they know how knowledge is organized, how to find information, and how to use information in such a way that others can learn from them. They are people prepared for lifelong learning, because they can always find the information needed for any task or decision at hand." The abilities to access, comprehend, use, and evaluate information have become the skills people must develop in order to function in our current world. *The Standards for 21st-Century Learners* (2009) outline the skills, dispositions, and responsibilities of students to be truly information literate in today's society, including the ability to inquire, think critically, draw conclusions, share information, make informed decisions, and apply knowledge to new situations. School library reference services play a particularly important role in fostering information literacy through the process of information inquiry, which involves the provision of information, instruction, and direction. (Figure 1.2 more completely explains the information inquiry process as it relates to student learning.)

Figure 1.2: The Information Inquiry Process as It Relates to Student Learning

At the onset of the information inquiry process, the student will:

Identify a Need or Problem
> *Be inquisitive about a wide range of topics, issues, and problems.*
> *Recognize the need for accurate and complete information.*
> *Brainstorm to focus the topic and formulate research questions.*

Once the topic is focused and the questions formulated, the student will:

Seek Appropriate Resources
> *Identify potential sources of information (print, electronic, community, etc.).*
> *Utilize effective research problem-solving strategies.*
> *Evaluate sources for appropriateness (reading level, biases, etc.).*

(continues)

Figure 1.2 (continued)

After the resources have been identified and evaluated, the student will:

Gather Information

> *Read, view, and hear a wide variety of appropriate materials.*
> *Gain background knowledge about the topic.*
> *Begin to build in-depth knowledge regarding certain aspects of the topic.*

As the material is being read, viewed, and heard, the student will:

Analyze Information

> *Skim and scan for keywords and major ideas.*
> *Determine the accuracy, relevance, and reliability of the information.*
> *Differentiate between fact and opinion, agreement, disagreement, etc.*
> *Identify biases, points of view, and cultural diversity.*

After analyzing the information, the student will:

Interpret and Synthesize Information

> *Summarize and paraphrase the information.*
> *Draw conclusions based on collected information.*
> *Create new information to replace inaccurate, misleading information as required.*
> *Integrate new information with prior knowledge.*
> *Logically organize and sequence the information.*
> *Apply information into critical thinking and problem solving to complete the task.*

Following the summarization of the information, the student will:

Communicate Information

> *Select a presentation format appropriate for the purpose and audience.*
> *Document sources using an appropriate format.*

To properly assess the learning process and identify areas needing further development and practice, the student will:

Evaluate Process and Product

> *Conduct an on-going evaluation by revising, improving, and updating the process and product as required.*
> *Determine if the project or process met the defined need(s).*
> *Determine what new skills/knowledge was gained.*

Information Inquiry, Standards for the 21st-Century Learner, and the Common Core Curriculum Standards

Education in the United States since the 1980s has largely been based on setting national standards for what students should know and be able to do at each grade level. Establishing standards for the purpose of ensuring that students develop lifelong information skills has not been excluded from this effort. Based on the 21st-Century Skills Framework, the American Association of School Librarians (AASL) developed the *Standards for the 21st-Century Learner* (2007) and *Standards for the 21st-Century Learner in Action* (2008), which address four main goals for learners:

1. Inquire, think critically, and gain knowledge.
2. Draw conclusions, make informed decisions, apply knowledge to new situations, and create new knowledge.
3. Share knowledge and participate ethically and productively as members of our democratic society.
4. Pursue personal and aesthetic growth.

The AASL national standards document *Empowering Learners: Guidelines for School Library Media Programs* (2009) outlines specific areas and activities for media centers in support of 21st-century learning goals. According to *Empowering Learners* (2009), "The mission of the school library media program is to ensure that students and staff are effective users of ideas and information. The school librarian empowers students to be critical thinkers, enthusiastic readers, skillful researchers, and ethical users of information by collaborating with students and teachers; providing instruction in information skills; providing access to materials in all formats; providing instruction and resources that reflect the current information environment; and providing leadership in the school educational program" (8).

Over the past several years, the National Governors Association has led a nationwide initiative to provide a clear and consistent curriculum framework for what students should know and be able to do to be prepared for college and work. To date, 45 of the 50 states have adopted the Common Core Standards (CCS), which currently outlines the P–12 curriculum for English Language Arts, Literacy in History/Social Studies, Science, and Technical Subjects. The adoption of these standards certainly has an impact on school libraries. Seven key points describe what it takes for a student to be college and career ready under the CCS: demonstrate independence; build strong content knowledge; respond to demands of audience, task, purpose, and discipline; comprehend as well as critique; value evidence; use technology and digital media strategically and capably; and come to understand other perspectives and cultures. The Common Core Standards also require students to be able to read and comprehend complex text in their content areas and require students to research to find the answer to questions. Information-inquiry skills are deeply embedded in these standards and offer the school librarian an open door to collaborate with teachers in the content areas and to become the information leader in their schools. To facilitate the role of school librarians in integrating the CCS into the school library program, the AASL has developed a

"Crosswalk of the Common Core Standards and the Standards for the 21st-Century Learner" so that school administrators, teachers, and school librarians can see how these standard documents are aligned.

Research Problem-Solving Processes and Models

Our complex, global society continues to expand at a rate beyond the capacity of individuals to comprehend. Access, evaluation, organization, and use of information are critical to ease the burden of change and to assist humanity in navigating its course toward the future. It is imperative that students possess the skills required to learn efficiently and effectively. By discussing research problem-solving strategies explicitly, it is more likely that these processes will be transferred to future research problem-solving situations.

The following three processes or models are widely accepted and used as problem-solving strategies in schools: Information Seeking by Carol Kuhlthau, the Big6 Information Problem-Solving Model by Michael Eisenberg and Robert Berkowitz, and the Research Process by Barbara Stripling and Judy Pitts. (Figure 1.3 provides a brief overview of these three models.)

Carol Kuhlthau's six-stage model of the Information Seeking process conceptualizes the construction of meaning through active participation with information resources. This model encourages an in-depth focus that enables students

---

Figure 1.3: Overview of Three Research or Problem-Solving Models or Processes: Information Seeking, Big6™ Information Problem Solving, Research Process

Information Seeking Kuhlthau	Big6™ Information Problem Solving Eisenberg and Berkowitz	Research Process Stripling and Pitts
Task initiation	Task identification	Choose broad topic
Topic selection		Overview of topic
		Narrow the topic
Formulation of focus	Information seeking strategies	Develop purpose
Exploration		Formulate question
		Plan for research
Collection	Location and access	Analyze, evaluate
	Information use	Evaluate evidence
Presentation	Synthesis	Make conclusions
Assessment	Evaluation	Create, present
		Reflection

Figure 1.4: Carol Kuhlthau's Information Seeking Process: Affective, Cognitive, Sensorimotor Learning

STAGE	Affective	Cognitive	Sensorimotor
Task Initiation	Uncertainty	General; Vague Thoughts	Recognizing one's information need
Topic Selection	Optimism	Scheduling or Planning	Identifying one's search problem
Exploration	Confusion; Frustration	Being informed about topic	Investigating scope of topic
Formulation	Ease accompanying clarity	Narrowing of topic focus	Formulating a search question
Collection	Sense of direction and confidence	Defining, supporting focus	Gathering notes
Presentation	Satisfied or Dissatisfied	More focused comprehension	Completing a report

to seek more relevant information and produce a product of higher quality. Kuhlthau states, "Living in the information age requires people to go beyond the ability to locate information and requires competence in seeking meaning and understanding. Students need to internalize the process of learning from information. They need to develop competency in deciding what is the best information for them and what is enough information for their ongoing process" (1997, 711). (Figure 1.4 displays this process as it relates to affective, cognitive, and sensorimotor learning.)

One recent, well-known information problem-solving model is the Big6 approach by Michael Eisenberg and Robert Berkowitz. This process describes the six thinking steps one goes through any time there is an information problem to be solved. They describe the strategy students use as "'Brainstorm and narrow' in which students brainstorm all possible information sources to meet the task and then critically determine the best sources for completing the particular task. (An overview of the Big6 problem-solving model is displayed in Figure 1.5 on page 12.)

The Super3 Information problem solving model was adapted from the Big6 to be used with P–2 students. The Super3 uses a simple three-step process to guide young children through the inquiry process.

Plan
- What do I need to do?
- What information do I need to do it?
- Write a list of questions.

Figure 1.5: Overview of the Big6 Information Problem-Solving Model (Michael Eisenberg and Robert Berkowitz)

The Big6 Information Problem-Solving Model

Task Definition
> *Define the problem.*
> *Identify the information.*
> *These questions should be asked prior to beginning the search:*
>> *What type of information do you need to solve your problem? Do you need current or historical materials? Do you need many or few sources?*

Information Seeking Strategies
> *Determine the range of possible resources.*
> *Evaluate the different possible sources to determine priorities.*
> *Determine what sources of information are available.*
> *Be cognizant of the need to tailor the amount of information to meet specific needs.*

Location and Access
> *Locate sources.*
> *Find information within sources.*

Use of Information
> *Engage.*
> *Extract relevant information (requires the majority of time).*
> *Note sources used; produce accurate citations.*

Synthesis
> *Organize information from multiple sources.*
> *Present information in an appropriate format.*

Evaluation
> *Judge the process or product.*

Do
- Where can I find what I need?
- Read, listen, view, and touch.
- Write notes.

Organize your information.
Make something to show what you learned.
Cite your sources.

Review
- Did I do what I was supposed to do?
- Should I do something before I turn it in?
- Do I feel good about what I did?

The Research Process developed by Barbara Stripling and Judy Pitts connects information handling and use with subject matter that is essential for learning to occur. Stripling and Pitts discovered that students have little prior knowledge of the information-seeking process, have fragmented understandings of subject knowledge, and that students do not understand that their information-seeking knowledge depends on content knowledge and vice versa. As a result, school librarians should plan instruction to specifically assist students in attaining these skills. Learning experiences should be viewed holistically, recognizing that one area (i.e., the information search process) can support other areas (i.e., content knowledge) and so forth. As Pitts noted, "There are many different, acceptable paths to the same end. Every . . . [student seemed] to have a different approach to working on a research assignment and organizing information. Each system worked well, but if everyone had been ordered to use one specific approach many students would have found themselves incredibly frustrated" (23).

Numerous additional information problem-solving research models and processes have been developed and can be extremely valuable and useful in developing school library reference services. Information problem solving and critical thinking involve the application, analysis, synthesis, and evaluation of information to construct personal meaning. Without this ability, students cannot go beyond the mere collection of information in order to weave information threads together into the creation of knowledge. Our role as school librarians is to encourage the appropriate problem-solving research processes, as well as critical thinking, in order to lead students to information. Ultimately self-directed learners lead themselves to knowledge from that information.

The Information-Seeking Process and Developmental Issues

As many of us know from direct experience, searching for and finding the information we need using online tools is not always an easy process. This task is sometimes made difficult for young students because a child's developmental level in their cognitive, literacy, and technical abilities presents a barrier to using the Internet to find information. Cognitively speaking, children have trouble with hierarchically structured information sites that require a specific sequence of navigation behaviors and find unstructured information environments containing distracting information links difficult to understand. Furthermore, children's preference for visual browsing for information over strategic keyword searching leads to longer, more circuitous searches with mixed success. Because their literacy skills are not well developed, children have trouble with tasks such as reading directions, spelling, and formulating appropriate words for keyword or phrase searching. They also have no knowledge or awareness of how to evaluate information resources they find. Finally, because their psychomotor skills are not well formed, children may not have developed the skills to use computer navigation tools and/or the technical expertise such as copying and pasting information to files saved on discs to manage information effectively. According to Todd (1998) children's developmental issues lead to ineffective use of information technologies for finding information if there is not appropriate intervention. The school media specialist plays a key role in developing students' information-seeking skills. For these reasons, among many others, the role of the media specialist in developing students' information skills is crucial if they are to succeed in the 21st-century learning environment and are the reasons for schools to establish comprehensive information literacy programs with the school library as the program's center.

Reference and the Technology Connection

Less than two decades ago information sources were synonymous with print materials. It is now an anomaly to use only printed resources in the realm of reference work. Librarians are now faced with the decision of which format to choose when purchasing information sources for their school. Electronic sources often times provide 24/7 information access to students and staff whereas print resources typically are noncirculating and must be used within the confines of the school media center. Students today are digital natives and prefer electronic resources over print resources. Many school librarians are opting to purchase more electronic resources instead of traditional reference materials. Publishers are following the digital preference by offering more popular reference materials in both electronic and print formats, while others have abandoned print in exchange for electronic. In the past, the Digital Divide was defined in terms of access to electronic information by people of different economic classes. In the 21st century, there is access to information on the Internet in schools and public libraries but the use of Internet filters often restricts access to illegal or controversial information resources. One of the most significant Digital Divides is now generational, and refers to the differences between the ways people born before 1977 access information compared with those born after 1977. It can also refer to the Western-adult bias inherent in the design of information search tools and resources, which presents an obstacle for nonadults and non-Westerners in their information search process.

Although reference services are changing in dynamic ways for school librarians, their essence, the provision of assistance to students seeking information, remains stable. The process of reference services is changing; the goal (the answer) remains constant. Technologies have made it possible to reach that goal faster and with more efficiency. The rapid growth and availability of information in electronic form is transforming the entire role of the school librarian and reference services as well. It has created a whole new range of options for finding and delivering information desired by students. With all the technologies available in our current global world, why are reference services still needed? They are required to determine, among the tons of information, the ounce necessary and useful for the student. They are required to assist students in learning how to access, organize, evaluate, and use information, learn how to learn, and become information literate. Ironically, technology has actually increased the student's need for assistance and reference services. With this in mind, school librarians face an opportunity and challenge—not an easy, but a necessary one—in response to the technological, societal changes of our modern times.

Conclusion

The three elements necessary for the reference process are the information/direction, the student, and the answer. One critical element concerning reference sources and services in today's technological society is information literacy. School librarians should foster information literacy, defined as the ability to access, comprehend, use, and evaluate information. School librarians should engage students in the process of information inquiry to help them learn how to learn and become lifelong learners. Reference work for the school librarian is a diverse variety of activities that can be viewed under the two headings of provision of information, and instruction or direction. What the school librarian does with regard to reference work is to answer questions, to assist in leading students to information. In order to efficiently and effectively conduct reference services, the school librarian should possess three things: knowledge of the collection, effective communication skills, and competence in selecting, organizing, and evaluating resources. The reference process consists of five basic steps that should be used as a guideline when conducting reference services: a need for information, a question, a search for information, an answer or response, and an evaluation.

Reference sources and services are constantly changing in response to new societal and technological developments in our information-hungry society. There exists an increased importance and availability of information. There is no doubt that expanding electronic applications will continue to contribute to the importance of reference and information services. It is argued that new electronic resources will also lead to an expansion of the guidance and instructional role of school librarians in the years ahead. School libraries and reference services are intended to enrich society and contribute to students' efforts to learn. The challenge is ours.

Useful Web Sites

AASL—Crosswalk of the Common Core Standards and the Standards for the 21st-Century Learner
> http://www.ala.org/aasl/guidelinesandstandards/commoncorecrosswalk
> *Explains the alignment of Common Core Standards and Standards for the 21st-Century Learner*

AASL—Learning for Life
> http://www.ala.org/aasl/guidelinesandstandards/learning4life
> *Companion for Empowering Learners Standards of School Media Centers publication*

AASL—Standards for the 21st-Century Learner
> http://www.ala.org/aasl/guidelinesandstandards/learningstandards/standards
> *Documents related to AASL Standards for the 21st-Century Learner*

Information Age Inquiry

    http://www.virtualinquiry.com/index.html

    A comprehensive site maintained by Indiana University–Purdue University Indianapolis devoted to information age inquiry concepts, instructional models, tools, and examples

Kuhlthau's Information Search Process and Guided Inquiry

    http://comminfo.rutgers.edu/~kuhlthau/information_search_process.htm

    http://comminfo.rutgers.edu/~kuhlthau/guided_inquiry.htm

    Wonderful overviews of the Information Search Process and Guided Inquiry Model, including a PowerPoint presentation by Carol Kuhlthau

The Big6 and Super3

    http://www.big6.com/

    Official site for the Big6 and Super3 information inquiry models

WebTools4U2Use

    http://webtools4U2use.wikispaces.com

    Web 2.0 Tools and school library applications

Chapter 2

Selection, Evaluation, and Maintenance of the Reference Collection

Introduction

The digital information revolution has resulted in the most marked changes in the types of reference sources and services used in the school library. Nowadays, the reference collection occupies at least two places in the library—on bookshelves in a separate section and on the school library Web page. The continuous transformation of references sources and services from a print-based medium to a mix of print and electronic formats has had a significant impact on the selection and evaluation of materials and how they are updated and maintained in the library.

Regardless of the format reference materials take, the primary consideration is providing teachers and students with easy access to a high-quality collection. How does a school librarian know what reference materials are needed in the school library? How does he or she know if a reference resource is good, bad, or indifferent? How does she decide if the reference resource should be in print or electronic format, or both? Following the rule that a good reference source is one that serves to answer a question, the focus of this chapter is effective selection and evaluation of reference resources for school libraries. As in most professional activities carried out by the school librarian, effective collection development is done collaboratively. In explaining the effective selection and evaluation of library reference materials, it is important to recall a principle in *Empowering Learners: Guidelines for School Library Media Programs*, which states, "The school librarian collaborates with the teaching staff to develop an up-to-date collection of print and digital resources in multiple genres that appeals to differences in age, gender, ethnicity, reading abilities, and information needs" (AASL, 2009, 38).

What is a reference source? Broadly speaking, it can be defined as materials, from book to computer to periodical to photograph, that can be found anywhere in the library or online. A narrow definition restricts the term to sources specifically designed to be consulted for definite items of information rather than to be examined consecutively. Reference resources may include Web sites, but although they may be a popular tool for locating information, Internet search engines are not considered reference resources because they retrieve a number of information resources and not a definite item of information. The role of search engines in reference services will be addressed later in the book.

Reference sources can be divided into two main classes: 1) compilations that furnish information directly (encyclopedias, dictionaries, almanacs, handbooks, yearbooks, biographical sources, directories, atlases); and 2) compilations that refer to other sources containing information, merely indicating places in which information can be found (bibliographies and indexes).

Adequate and appropriate selection and evaluation of reference materials involves consideration of specific criteria and aids or tools that may be useful in collection development. (Both types of reference sources are explained in detail in the following chapters.) School librarians have a multitude of tasks; one critical task is the selection and evaluation of reference materials—print and electronic. Without the proper tools, expertise, or good judgment to accomplish this task, students' informational needs may remain unanswered.

What Do You Need?—The Selection Process

Selection is the process of deciding what materials to add to the school library media collection. In choosing reference resources, a school librarian plans and carries out certain activities that culminate in selection decisions. These activities include identifying and assessing evaluative information about reference materials, examining the resources, and providing ways to involve others in the selection process. Meeting curriculum needs is a major criterion for placing items in the media center collection. School librarians should review state and national curriculum standards and textbooks used by all teachers on a regular basis. They should also regularly assess teachers' instructional methods and become aware of particular research and other assignments given by teachers. Above all, collaboration with teachers on assignments using information resources is crucial for continuous improvement in developing an effective reference collection. One of the most important tasks of a school librarian is to help students and teachers find the best materials available—in all formats—to support teaching and learning.

All materials, including reference, should meet the criteria of the library media center selection policy. Selection policies are vital because they explain the process followed and the priorities established before any resource is purchased and placed in the school library collection. A selection policy will state the selection aids used in choosing resources. Numerous tools or aids review new reference publications. Remember, however, that selection is not completely the responsibility of the school librarian. It also belongs to administrators, teachers, students, parents, and community members. Input from these people is essential for a useful and appropriate reference collection.

A number of tools or aids are available to assist the school library media specialist in deciding which resources are needed for possible inclusion in the reference collection. Reviews are critical to suitable selection and evaluation of reference materials. However, the school librarian's informed judgment in the selection of materials best suited to the library and student population is of equal importance. Regardless of the situation, a thorough knowledge of the library's existing resources is imperative. There are numerous journals, guidebooks, and online sources to assist school librarians with the selection of print and electronic reference materials. Most journals contain reviews of electronic media as well as print sources; articles, columns, editorials, and other information are also included. The following are examples of effective selection tools or aids:

All Grade Levels:
- *American Libraries* (American Library Association)
  American Libraries magazine, available in both print and online formats, lists outstanding reference sources for small and medium-sized libraries. The Reference and User Services Association's (RUSA) Reference Sources Committee lists the best reference materials of the year online.
  http://americanlibrariesmagazine.org/
  http://www.ala.org/rusa/

- *American Reference Books Annual* (Libraries Unlimited, Inc.)
  American Reference Books Annual has been published annually since 1970 and is currently available in print and online formats, including annotations, reviews, and other commentary useful for selection and evaluation of reference materials for school librarians. The online version offers a 30-day trial subscription.
  http://www.arbaonline.com/

- *Booklist* (American Library Association)
  Booklist magazine is published semimonthly by the American Library Association and includes Reference Books Bulletin, which focuses specifically on reference resources for the school library. It reviews current books, videos, and software and provides monthly author/title indexes as well as semiannual cumulative indexes. *Booklist* online provides continuous access to these resources. The online version offers a free trial subscription.
  http://www.booklistonline.com/

- *The Horn Book Magazine* (The Horn Book, Inc.)
  The Horn Book Magazine is published bimonthly with a focus on children's resources, including reference materials. It also publishes reviews, articles, editorials, and columns related to children's literature. *The Horn Book Guide* is published annually and contains reviews of hardback and paperback books, including bibliographic information, size, age level, summary of content, and other pertinent information regarding the selection of elementary materials. *The Horn Book Guide* is also available online.
  http://hbook.com/

- *Library Media Connection* (Linworth Books/ABC-CLIO)
  Library Media Connection is a magazine that includes the publishers' two previous magazines, *Library Talk* and *The Book Report*. It provides integrated information for print and multimedia materials, innovative ideas, and practical tips and techniques (appropriate for all age levels). This inclusive magazine includes reviews of books, software, and other electronic resources written by professionals in the school library media field.
  http://www.librarymediaconnection.com

- *Internet@Schools* (Information Today, Inc.)
  Internet@Schools is available in print and online formats. It provides reviews of books, databases and online sources, hardware, and other technologies appropriate for K–12 school library media centers.
  http://www.internetatschools.com/

- *School Library Journal* (MediaSource Inc.)
  School Library Journal (SLJ) is a leading magazine for school librarians. One half of SLJ is dedicated to critical reviews of print and electronic resources. SLJ provides 12 issues per year; the December copy presents the editor's choices for Best Books of the Year. The SLJ companion Web site provides an archive of past issues, plus reviews, newsletters, and blogs, some of which do not require a subscription.
  http://www.schoollibraryjournal.com

- *A Guide to Reference Materials for School Libraries*, 6th ed. (Libraries Unlimited, Inc.)
  This print resource covers more than 2,000 titles and includes age and reading levels, digital and print formats, presentation styles, strengths and weaknesses, comparisons with other titles, citations, and reviews.

Primary and Elementary Grade Levels:
- Children's Core Collection (H. W. Wilson/EBSCO)
  Children's Core Collection online database provides a wide-ranging annotated listing of more than 13,000 of the best fiction and nonfiction books, new and established, written for children from preschool through sixth grade. A free trial subscription is available.
  http://www.ebscohost.com/academic/childrens-core-collection

Secondary Grade Levels:
- Best Books for Young Adults
  Best Books for Young Adults, compiled by the Young Adult Library Services Association, contains indexed, annotated lists of young adults books extending back to 1966. Titles are accessible by author, awards, and top ten lists.
  http://www.ala.org/yalsa/booklists/bbya

- The Middle and Junior High Core Collection (H. W. Wilson/EBSCO)
  The Middle and Junior High Core Collection online provides an annotated list of more than 9,000 fiction and nonfiction books for grades five through

eight published in the United States, Canada, and the United Kingdom, with annotations, subject headings, and reviews.
http://www.ebscohost.com/academic/middle-and-junior-high-core-collection

- The Senior High School Core Collection (H. W. Wilson/EBSCO)
The Senior High School Core Collection online database represents a well-balanced collection of more than 40,500 outstanding fiction and nonfiction titles essential to the senior high school library collection (grades 9 through 12).
http://www.ebscohost.com/academic/senior-high-core-collection

Web Sites:
- KidsClick.com (www.KidsClick.com)
KidsClick provides educational and fun software just for kids!

- Internet Public Library (http://www.ipl.org)
The IPL is maintained by a consortium of university library science programs and serves as a portal for authoritative Web resources for children and adults. There are separate sections for children and adults, online periodicals, and an alphabetical subject guide. The Reference area in the Kidspace section includes links such as: Homework Help, Dictionaries, Encyclopedias, and more.

Additional tools may include selection sources published by the American Library Association (http://www.ala.org), the Association for Educational Communications and Technology (http://www.aect.org), Gale Research (http://www .gale.com), H. W. Wilson/ EBSCO (http://www.ebscohost.com/wilson), and R. R. Bowker (http://www.bowker.com). Reviews from professional journals in major academic areas should be considered as well. Reference selection tools or aids serve to assist the school librarian in evaluating sources for possible inclusion into the library, as well as identifying gaps in the reference collection. However, these are merely aids; they can only assist if the school librarian has a complete knowledge of the collection and uses good judgment based on the existing resources and the needs of the community and students served.

How Do You Know If It's Good? —The Evaluation Process

A good reference source is one that serves to answer questions, and a bad reference source is one that fails to answer questions. Still another function as a school library media specialist is to continually evaluate the quality of the library's reference collection. By using appropriate evaluation tools and criteria, the school librarian is better able to judge whether a particular source meets the needs of the student population. While evaluation criteria were originally developed for printed sources, the evaluation of electronic information considers many of the same elements, with several added components. Much is subjective when judging any kind of resource. However, the following criteria (appropriate for both print and electronic information) will assist school librarians in evaluating reference resources of value to meet students' informational needs.

CONTENT SCOPE

Identifying the scope of material presented is the basic breadth and depth question of what is covered and in what detail. The scope should reflect the purpose of the source and its intended audience. Has the author or editor accomplished what was intended? How current are the contents? Aspects of scope include subject, geographical, and time period coverage. Evaluating scope includes reviewing topical aspects of the subject about which the resource is focused and noting if there are any key omissions from the subject area. For printed materials, the statement of purpose is generally found in the preface, introduction, or contents; for an electronic site, one should look for the stated purpose on the site, along with any limitations that may apply, and site comprehensiveness. Information about CD-ROMs and DVDs can usually be found in the publisher's or vendor's descriptive materials.

ACCURACY, AUTHORITY, AND BIAS

Indicators of authority include the education and experience of the authors, editors, and contributors, as well as the reputation of the publisher or sponsoring agency. Typically, it is easier to evaluate the authority of printed reference sources, because statements of authorship and lists of references can be more easily identified. On the other hand, it is at times extremely difficult to discover who actually provided the information on an electronic site. Some items to look for include who provided the information, why, and explicit statements of authority. Objectivity and fairness of a source are also important considerations. Does the author or contributor have biases? How reliable are the facts presented? Many times this can be assessed by examining the coverage of controversial issues and the balance in coverage given to various subjects. Was the site developed as a means of advertisement or as scholarly material? The creator of the information may serve as an indicator of biases on electronic sites.

ARRANGEMENT AND PRESENTATION

Printed sources arrange entries in a particular sequence, such as alphabetical, chronological, or classified. If the sequence is familiar, the user may be able to directly find the information sought, rather than using an index. The flexibility of the reference source is typically enhanced by the availability of indexes offering different types of access to the information. Physical makeup, binding, illustrations, and layout are concerns with print resources. Presentation issues regarding electronic information include page or site layout, clarity or intuitiveness of the site's organizational design, and help or example sections. Some things to look for include appropriate audience, use of graphics, navigational links, and a table of contents.

RELATION TO SIMILAR WORKS

Newly published material may have different types of relationships to sources already in your school library collection. These need to be taken into account in assessing the potential value of the new resource to the collection. What will this resource add to the current collection? Regarding electronic materials, it is important to assess the extent to which the content corresponds (time period covered, more information provided, etc.).

TIMELINESS AND PERMANENCE

Printed resources are often considered to be out of date before they reach the student. All sources should be checked for currency. Sometimes relevant information on an electronic site can be located in a document header or footer. Information to observe includes posting and revision dates, policy statements for information maintenance, and link maintenance. It is also significant to recognize that there is no guarantee that a particular file of information will reside in the same location today as it did yesterday. A good strategy is to note the date and time a site is visited if one intends to use the information and a citation is taken.

ACCESSIBILITY/DIVERSITY

Reference resources must be accessible to the entire student population regardless of linguistic or physical limitations. This criterion considers how well the item meets the needs of linguistically, culturally, and intellectually varied learners and learners with special needs. In addition, the overall collection must be developed to provide the school community with inclusive information from different cultural perspectives. School libraries may have a number of reference items covering the same content that present information in different formats, languages, or reading levels in order to meet the needs of diverse learners.

COST

Sometimes budget, rather than student need, may determine whether a particular reference source is purchased. The cost of print materials and those in distributed electronic form are similar, in that a copy is acquired for in-house use in the school library, and the purchase or subscription price buys unlimited access to the contents of the resource. However, online costs may vary widely. In assessing the cost, the school librarian must attempt to determine if the price is appropriate in relation to the needs of the students, as well as anticipated frequency and length of use. Also, the school librarian must consider licenses for software and other related issues. In the case of electronic materials, it is important to consider the cost of hardware and maintenance as well.

Collection Organization and Maintenance

The print reference collection typically occupies a specific section in the school library near the circulation desk. Many libraries have transformed the print reference area into a reading area to provide students with a comfortable place to use reference sources that do not circulate. To extend the reference collection outside library walls, school libraries often provide a separate reference page on their Web sites that provides ready access to electronic reference resources provided by the school.

Whether reference sources are in print or electronic format, accurate arrangement and maintenance of the reference collection is necessary in order to provide convenience and ease of use by the school librarian, as well as the student population. A reference collection that is unplanned, disorganized, or not weeded appropriately may prove ineffective and unresponsive to the information needs of students. A systematic basis for reviewing resources, weeding, as well as adding new materials to the reference collection should exist. As a school librarian, what is already in the collection and what is actually needed for effective reference work by students must be taken into account. Factors affecting weeding of reference materials are similar to the total school library collection: age or currency of material, frequency of use, relevance, physical condition, format, and space availability. It is more important to have a small but relevant and up-to-date collection of materials than a large collection that is neither useful nor of good quality.

Some reference materials, obviously, become outdated. If so, a school library media specialist should consider the following basic guidelines: print encyclopedias should be replaced every five years (and the old ones not sent to a classroom, but discarded); pure science books, print format (except botany and natural history), are out of date within five years; any books dealing with technology should be replaced every five years (or more often); print information on inventions and medicine is dated within five years; print psychology, history, business, and education sources become dated in ten years; and newspapers and magazines, print format, should be kept up to five years (although most are now purchased either on CD-ROM or online). Where should these withdrawn materials go? If resources are weeded due to a change in curriculum, it may be beneficial to relocate them to another library. Otherwise, weeded materials should be destroyed. (Personally take them to a dumpster and throw them in!)

Current school library reference collections include sources in a variety of formats, from print materials to online sources. The school library media specialist must decide what format to purchase, as well as whether to obtain particular materials in more than one reading level, language, and format. Although varying formats may overlap in content, they may differ in access capabilities. School librarians have more options than ever before in creating a reference collection that is adequate and appropriate for the school library, community, and students served.

Decisions in collection development include whether to buy new titles, to buy new editions of titles already in the collection, to buy the source in CD-ROM or DVD format, or whether to contract with vendors for online access. Maintaining this diverse reference collection is an ongoing process. Regular inventory of the reference collection and review of individual print and electronic resources are required to identify areas that need to be updated or strengthened.

There are a variety of possible arrangements of reference materials. The arrangement will depend on the library, the students served, alignment with the curriculum, as well as personal preferences of the school library media specialist. At the elementary level, reference instruction continues to use print sources because of the difficulty young children experience in navigating the Internet. However, use of print resources decreases as the level of education increases because older students can make effective use of the sophisticated search interfaces and wide variety of reference resources available online.

Table 2.1: General guidelines for replacing reference materials	
Print encyclopedias	*5 years*
Science books, print format, except botany and natural history	*5 years*
Technology related	*5 years*
Inventions and medicine, print format	*5 years*
Print psychology, history, business, and education	*10 years*
Newspapers and magazines, print format	*5 years*

Blanche Woolls remarks, "It is time to consider ways to make the entire school the library" (75). As an example, the Learning Commons model for school libraries embraces this holistic vision, in which the library is a flexible space functioning as a learning hub for information inquiry and technology. School libraries based on this model have reference materials on mobile shelving units and expansive virtual reference resources. As another example, schools that have adopted a whole language curriculum and teach curriculum across the school need to have reference materials away from the central library collection. In both of these scenarios, the school librarian must formulate and implement a plan for keeping track of materials such that they can be located quickly and easily. If this option is not currently feasible, one possibility for grouping materials is to maintain a classified arrangement regardless of type. Another alternative is to assemble types of resources together, such as encyclopedias, directories, ready-reference, and the like. Although it might be difficult to integrate sources requiring special equipment, such as computer workstations, as wireless technology develops school librarians will be able to provide students with reference sources with increasing access and flexibility.

Conclusion

In order to create and maintain a school reference collection that meets the informational needs of students, effective selection and evaluation of resources by the school librarian is essential. Several considerations are important with regard to the selection of reference materials: 1) knowing about the school, the school community, and the student population (input from teachers, staff, and students is also vital), as these individuals have content experience/knowledge that a school library media specialist may not have; 2) continuous collaboration with teachers and eliciting the expert advice of the school's faculty members and drawing on their experience and knowledge; and 3) keeping a record of questions asked or research requests. Remember as well that the selection process is a highly individualized one. No two school librarians are alike; student needs differ from school to school. Attention should be given not only to known requests but also to anticipated demands.

Because of the high cost of many reference materials, it is critical that effective evaluation of reference resources occurs by the school library media specialist. Although much judgment is subjective, tools or aids and specific criteria are available to assist with appropriate evaluation of reference sources. In the technologically oriented world of today, evaluation is even more complex and diverse—and much more vital. A thorough knowledge of existing resources, as well as the community and school population served, is crucial to successful evaluation of reference materials. Additionally, experience and practice is significant in making correct decisions. As explained by William A. Katz, "In time the beginner becomes a veteran. And veteran [school librarians] never quit; or are fired, or die. They simply gain fame as being among the wisest people in the world. One could do worse" (3).

PART 2

Nuts
and
Bolts

Chapter 3
Bibliographies

Introduction

A bibliography brings order out of chaos. Simply stated, a bibliography is a list of materials. More thorough definitions of the term *bibliography* are: 1) the history, identification, or description of writings or publications; and 2) a list of descriptive or critical works of writing related to a particular subject, period, or author; a list written by an author or printed by a publishing house. Bibliographies are useful tools; they can tell a user the author of a work, who published the material and when, how much it costs, and so on. The basic purpose remains the same, whether the format is print or electronic.

Bibliographic control refers to two kinds of access to information: bibliographic access (Does the work exist?) and physical access (Where can the work be found?). Providing bibliographic and physical access is achieved through bibliographies, library catalogs, and bibliographic utilities. Bibliographies list materials (or parts of materials) regardless of location; library catalogs list works located in a given library (or libraries); bibliographic utilities serve both functions. Bibliographic utilities are information vendors who provide a centralized database for libraries to catalog, share, and retrieve bibliographic records according to national or international bibliographic standards. Bibliographies and library catalogs can be current or retrospective. Current bibliographies and library catalogs list works close to the time at which they are published. Retrospective bibliographic sources cover materials published during an earlier time.

A universal bibliography (although it is currently a nonexistent entity) would include everything published from the beginning through the present. Time, territory, subject, language, or form would not limit it. Access to the world's information is definitely nearer. It is doubtful that a complete bibliography will be seen in the immediate future; however, almost complete is a reality. This phenomenon is accomplished by having online access to national bibliographies; an example being the Online Computer Library Center (OCLC) found online at www.oclc.org (OCLC First Search at www.oclc .org/oclc/menu/fs.htm).

Bibliographies can be divided into several different types: national bibliographies, trade bibliographies, library catalogs, union catalogs, and subject catalogs. National bibliographies list materials published in a particular country and are often the product of the government. Current national bibliographies usually appear weekly or monthly with annual or multiyear cumulations. The United States' national bibliography is called the National Union Catalog (NUC). It lists all works that are cataloged by the Library of Congress and other members of the system.

Trade bibliographies are commercial publications that include the necessary information to select and purchase recently published materials. Works such as textbooks, government documents, encyclopedias, and dissertations are not included in trade bibliographies. A well-known bibliography of this type is *Books in Print* (BIP). BIP is limited to books available for purchase and contains only printed books (hardbound and paperback).

Library catalogs list materials in the collection of a particular library (such as a school library media center). Because of the prevalence of online catalogs, many libraries can now provide this information to both local and remote users. These catalogs may also list the collections of other libraries—school library media centers, public libraries, academic libraries, and so on.

Union catalogs identify the materials held in more than one library. Through bibliographic utilities such as WorldCat, Library of Congress, and the Internet, it is possible to view holdings in thousands of libraries around the world. The geographic area covered may vary from local to multinational.

Subject bibliographies are lists of materials that relate to a specific topic; they are intended for those researching special areas. Hundreds of subject bibliographies exist; many follow the same pattern of organization and presentation. Various disciplines and large areas of knowledge have their own bibliographies (see "Examples of Subject Bibliographies").

Examples of Subject Bibliographies

Bibliographies of the War of American Independence
> http://www.army.mil/cmh-pg/reference/revbib/revwar.htm
> *This Web site provides bibliographies that were originally produced by the U.S. Army Center of Military History, Historical Resources Branch.*

Classic Bibliographies Online
> *This site includes Literature Bibliographies, the Ancient Mediterranean, Greek and Roman History, and Greek and Latin Language.*

Dream Gate and Electric Dreams
> http://dreamgate.com/dream/bibs/
> *This Web site offers a collection of bibliographies of dream researchers, clinicians, dream workers, anthropologists, and other dream-concerned individuals and groups.*

Index of Native American Bibliography Resources on the Internet
> http://www.hanksville.org/NAresources/indices/NAbib.html
> *This site is offered by the Internet School Library Media Center, providing bibliographies, directories to pages of tribes, history and historical documents, periodicals, and general links.*

Online Chaucer Bibliographies
> http://englishcomplit.unc.edu/chaucer/chbib.htm
> *This site provides an organized navigation aid for Chaucer resources on the Web, including Chaucer Pages, Chaucer Works, Life and Times, and so forth.*

Evaluation and Selection

Evaluation of Print Bibliographies

AUTHORITY
- The compilers or authors should possess the academic backgrounds or academic structure to justify their roles in writing a bibliography.
- Look for reputable publishers of bibliographies, such as Brodart and H. W. Wilson.
- It is important to verify the reputation of lesser-known publishers.

FREQUENCY
- The source should be current when that is the purpose of the bibliography.

ORGANIZATION
- The source should be organized in a clear, user-friendly fashion, with indexes that complement the arrangement.
- Explicit explanations regarding how to use the work should be included.

SCOPE
- The scope should be stated in the introduction or preface.
- Consult guides to the reference works that give concise, unambiguous descriptions of coverage, accuracy, and intent.

When evaluating bibliographies in print format, the following criteria should be used: authority, frequency, organization, and scope. Authority relates to the qualifications of the compiler or the author. The compilers or authors should possess the educational backgrounds and/or academic structure to justify their roles in writing a bibliography. As with all reference areas, reputable publishers of bibliographies exist, such as R. R. Bowker, Brodart, and H. W. Wilson. It is advisable to verify the reputation of lesser-known publishers through review tools and aids. A bibliography should be current when this is the purpose of the bibliography. Currency also refers to the delay between the date of publication of the material to be listed and the time at which it entered in the bibliography. Frequency, or the number of times per year the bibliography is updated, is most applicable when selecting current as opposed to retrospective bibliographies. It is important to note that often the same work has a different updating schedule in each of its formats. Bibliographies will vary widely in organization or arrangement. However, all bibliographies should be organized in a clear, user-friendly fashion with indexes that complement the arrangement. In addition, the compiler should offer explicit explanations regarding how to effectively use the work. Bibliographies must be as complete as possible within their stated purposes. In the introduction or preface, the compiler should state the scope of the bibliography. It is also valuable to consult guides to the reference works that give concise and unambiguous descriptions of coverage, accuracy, and intent.

Evaluation of Electronic Bibliographies

The following criteria should be considered when evaluating electronic bibliographies.

CONTENT
- A high percentage of the content should be full-text.
- Images should be used to enhance the content.
- Basic and advanced search features should be available.
- Scope statement should be available.

VENDOR
- Customer Service and Support should be offered through a help desk or phone support.
- Training should be provided for staff and students.

STATISTICAL
- Reports on usage should be easily exported or printed.
- Results of reports should be easily interpreted.
- Type of reports may be determined by the vendor or library.

TECHNICAL
- Authentication—is username and password set by vendor or school?
- Access—is user access limited to the school day or anytime?
- Proxy/Firewall—are there complications for configuring the network proxy/firewall?

The selection of bibliographies for a school library media center situation depends on the needs—both known and anticipated—of the school, community, and student population served. Before selecting a specific bibliography, it is advisable to read the introduction and several entries. It may also be helpful to ask the following questions: Does the bibliography meet identified needs? Are the directions accurate and the explanations clear? Is the bibliography available in several formats? Is the coverage inclusive for the intended purposes? Is it evident why the items are included in the bibliography? Is the bibliography well organized and user friendly? Remain aware of the overall purpose of bibliographies—to provide information about the availability of materials, their costs, and whether they are recommended (although not all bibliographic tools include this element).

Basic Sources

There are several well-known, basic bibliographies for libraries. It is valuable and helpful to become familiar with these reference tools, although your school library media center situation may not require nor have the budget to purchase such resources.

The American Book Publishing Record (ABPR), published by R. R. Bowker, is a monthly publication that includes complete cataloging records for books as they are published.

The American Reference Books Annual (ARBA), an annual publication by Libraries Unlimited, analyzes more than 20,000 reference titles. This tool is limited to titles published or distributed in the United States and Canada. ARBA is comprehensive and includes annotations written by subject experts. ARBA is updated at the beginning of each month. Available in print and electronic formats (www.arbaonline.com).

Books in Print (BIP), published annually by R. R. Bowker, is a listing of books available from U.S. publishers. BIP includes more than one million citations; thousands of new titles are added annually. BIP is updated with the *Books in Print Supplement*, which appears approximately six months after the main volumes of BIP. *Children's Books in Print* includes more than 100,000 in-print titles as well as videos and audiocassettes. This bibliography is published annually. The online version of *Books in Print* includes Children's Books in Print, Global Books in Print, Spanish Books in Print, and Patron Books in Print (www.booksinprint.com).

Book Review Digest Plus is available online (http://www.ebscohost.com/academic/book-review-digest-plus). This bibliographic database contains more than 225,000 English language fiction and nonfiction titles, and over 118,000 new reviews are added each year.

Guide to Reference Books, an American Library Association publication, lists and annotates more than 1,000 titles that are arranged under main sections; it provides an inclusive index (http://www.guidetoreference.org/DynamicContent.aspx?ctype=21). The database is updated on an ongoing basis. It is available in print and online. They offer a free and subscription based service.

Guide to Reference Materials for School Library Media Centers, 6th ed., by Barbara Ripp Safford and published by Libraries Unlimited, contains bibliographic descriptions of over 700 reference titles for school libraries arranged by subject.

Informational Picture Books for Children, by Patricia J. Cianciolo and published by the American Library Association, contains annotations for over 250 titles of nonfiction picture books including many reference books for young children.

Literary Market Place, published annually by R. R. Bowker, provides current data on publishers. It is available in print as well as online (http://www.literarymarket place.com) and features over 30,000 entries on books, companies, and periodicals, to name a few categories.

Of particular importance to school library media centers, the following examples of bibliographies may also be thought of as selection tools. There are numerous works of this nature; these are merely a sampling of bibliographies that are valuable for school library media centers. It is important to purchase these resources carefully, as they are essential for effective collection development.

Numerous bibliographies are available online at no cost. For example, many states currently have virtual libraries. These online libraries provide valuable information and are significant resources that should not be overlooked for school library media centers. Other examples of valuable online sources are Bookwire (www .bookwire.com) by R. R. Bowker, which claims to be the most comprehensive online information source and contains information on 20 million titles of print, e-books, and audio books; and the Internet Library for Librarians (www.itcompany.com/ inforetriever), which provides information about library vendors, publishers, booksellers, and distributors as well as an abundance of information regarding specific school library media and reference resources.

A wealth of information is at our fingertips; at times it may seem too much. Bibliographies, however, can organize this data into meaningful, valuable units—and eliminate chaos and provide order.

Webliography

Books in Print
> http://www.booksinprint.com
> *This is the largest Web-based bibliographic resource for professionals, including an authoritative and comprehensive database of more than five million books, audio books, and video titles. This site includes Children's Books in Print, Global Books in Print, Spanish Books in Print, and Patron Books in Print.*

Book Review Digest Plus
> http://www.ebscohost.com/academic/book-review-digest-plus
> *Via this Web site, one can retrieve book summaries, bibliographic data, full-text reviews, review excerpts, or basic citations encompassing more than 225,000 full-text reviews.*

BookWire
> http://www.bookwire.com
> *Bookwire makes it easier for people to discover, evaluate, order, and experience books. Powered by Bowker's Books in Print® database, Bookwire makes it easy to search and discover over 20 million book titles, including print, e-books, audio books, and more.*

Internet Library for Librarians
> http://www.itcompany.com/inforetriever
> *This Web site is a portal designed for librarians to locate Internet resources related to their profession.*

Literary Market Place
> http://www.literarymarketplace.com
> *This is a fee-based site and a worldwide resource for the book publishing industry.*

OCLC FirstSearch
> http://www.oclc.org/firstsearch/
> *This online service gives users access to a collection of reference databases; FirstSearch materials in your library's collection are highlighted in results from searches in dozens of leading databases.*

Online Computer Library Center (OCLC)
http://www.oclc.org
This Web site is a Worldwide Library Cooperative, offering OCLC Worldwide, Librarian's Toolbox, Resources, and more.

Chapter 4

Directories, Almanacs, Yearbooks, and Handbooks

Introduction

One person's trivia is another person's main interest. General reference sources such as factbooks, directories, almanacs, handbooks, and yearbooks primarily answer factual questions. *Ready-reference* is a term used to describe an information service in which librarians provide easy-to-locate facts in response to fairly simple questions. Ready-reference is all about facts. Although Internet search engines satisfy our most immediate needs for information, it is often necessary to use an authoritative source for finding facts. A fact book is a publication containing information organized in a systematic way. As stated in Dickens' *Hard Times*, "Now what I want is facts. . . . facts alone are wanted in life." A ready-reference question may only take a minute or two to answer; however, it may develop into a complex search. For example, a student who requests the address of a specific college may actually not only want the address, but also information about how to apply to the college and other related data. The purpose of this chapter is to provide an overview of these reference tools, their chief uses, selection procedures, considerations for evaluation, and examples of sources used in school library media centers.

Factbooks are general reference tools providing basic facts on particular topics such as countries, sports, or time periods. Factbooks are used to quickly answer basic questions about places, time periods, and specialized subjects. The arrangement of factbooks is typically determined by the subject matter. For example, a factbook on countries of the world might be arranged by region or alphabetically, while a factbook on current events might be arranged chronologically or categorically. Factbooks that focus on current information are often found in both print and online formats.

Directories are defined by the *ALA Glossary of Library and Information Science* as "a list of persons or organizations, systematically arranged, usually in alphabetic or classed order, giving address, affiliations, etc. for individuals, and address, officers, functions, and similar data for organizations" (Levine-Clark and Carter, 2012). This definition is a pure one; it should be noted that aside from directories themselves, numerous other ready-reference tools have sections devoted to directory information. Directories are used to locate and verify names of phenomena, as well as to match individuals with organizations. Students often wish to locate other people, experts, organizations, and institutions through addresses, phone numbers, zip codes, titles, names, and so on. Directories are the most rapid and effective method of obtaining this sort of information. Less obvious uses of directories include limited biographical information about an individual and information about an institution or political group. Because directories are closely concerned with humans and their organizations, they can serve numerous uses. Although directories can be divided into a number of categories, the following are six basic types: government, institutional, investment, local, professional, and trade and business. Because it is so easy and cost effective to update information available online, many organizations have ceased their print directories and now publish them only in an online format.

Almanacs, yearbooks, and handbooks provide factual information about numerous items, such as people, organizations, things, current and historical events, countries, governments, and statistical trends. Many other sources also offer this type of information; however, almanacs, yearbooks, and handbooks are more convenient sources of this data. Often these sources are single volumes that summarize and synthesize large amounts of information. Many of the most popular almanacs such as the *Old Farmer's Almanac* are available online.

An almanac is a resource that provides useful data and statistics related to countries, personalities, events, and subjects. It is a publication containing astronomical and meteorological data arranged according to days, weeks, and months of a given year, and often including a miscellany of other information. Almost every school library can benefit from having a general almanac. A paperbound edition of many almanacs costs less than $20. The most famous early almanac was Benjamin Franklin's *Poor Richard's Almanac*, published from 1732 to 1748. The *Old Farmer's Almanac* is an example of this type of almanac that currently continues to be published. Although almanacs can be extensive in geographical coverage, many of the best-known general almanacs are inclined toward a specific country or state. An almanac can answer questions such as the following: Where was George W. Bush born? What is the population of Oman? Which NCAA Division 1 team has won the most regular season games? How much saturated fat is in a pound of butter? What is the address of the American Embassy in Italy?

Yearbooks present facts and statistics for a single year (primarily the year preceding the publication date). Encyclopedias often issue yearbooks that supplement the main set and are fundamentally the review of a specific year. A yearbook's primary purpose is to record the year's activities by country, subject, or specialized area. A general yearbook is the place to find information on topics such as the winner of an athletic event of that year, an obituary for a notable person who died during the year, or the description of a catastrophe that occurred that particular year.

Handbooks are sometimes called manuals; they serve as guides to a particular subject. Often large amounts of information about a subject are compressed into a single volume. The content and organization of handbooks may vary widely. The basic purpose of handbooks is as ready-reference sources for given fields of knowledge. With a few exceptions, most handbooks have a limited scope. Their particular value is depth of information in a narrow field. There are countless handbooks available; school librarians should select specific ones based on ease of arrangement and amount of use. Handbooks provide answers to questions such as these: How do I cite references within the text in MLA format? Who wrote the poem, *The Raven*? Is single or double spacing used when writing a research paper? Who is known as the Greek goddess of love?

Facts that answer ready-reference questions are a major part of reference services in school library media centers. Providing ample, as well as suitable, resources of this type is essential for any school collection. Although certain factual information can be located in other reference sources, it is always beneficial to have basic factbooks, directories, almanacs, yearbooks, and handbooks (in all formats) available to meet the informational needs of students. Often students will expect quick and authoritative answers to their questions using an Internet search engine such as Google, but are often disappointed by the number of irrelevant results and annoying advertisements. If for this reason only, it is a wise choice that the reference section maintains a ready-reference collection containing these basic sources.

Evaluation and Selection

The general rules of evaluating any reference work are applicable to factbooks, directories, almanacs, yearbooks, and handbooks as well. To some degree, we all rely on what reference materials state as facts; however, these should be tested regularly. Is it a fact or an opinion? Is the fact no longer a fact? For instance, at one time in our history, it was a fact that the world was flat. Due to discoveries and experiments, this fact is no longer true—no longer a fact. An effective method of checking a fact is to find its original source. The reference source should clearly indicate where the information was obtained. The following criteria are useful in evaluating factbooks, directories, almanacs, yearbooks, and handbooks:

Scope: What exactly is covered? What organizations, geographic areas, or types of individuals are included in the resource? How comprehensive is the source within its stated scope? The title many times gives insight into the scope of a source; the preface (or introductory materials in electronic sources) will often provide even more detailed information.

Currency: What is the frequency of the publication? How often is it updated? Almanacs, yearbooks, and titles that are updated once a year typically overcome this dilemma; this is also true of online resources.

Accuracy: Accuracy is the single most important characteristic of works that present factual information. How is the information in the source updated? Numerous methods are used in updating records, such as verifying by telephone, examining public records, and so on. To test accuracy, one can read reviews, compare data from different sources, and rely on experts in the field. Many of these reference resources are composed, in part, of second-hand information. The statistics should be recent and from official sources; those sources should be identified. Reference works without documentation are of questionable validity.

Format: Are the entries clearly arranged, organized in a logical manner, and consistent throughout the source? Indexes are a significant factor in providing access to the information sources. The index in a fact source should be helpful, accurate, and consistent in style and terminology. A major consideration is the availability of the resource in electronic format. Electronic formats may contain more current information than their printed counterparts. Electronic versions can cumulate a number of years and eliminate the need to consult numerous volumes. Electronic sources can often be searched more efficiently. Keyword searching is helpful. By keyword searching, the exact names or titles need not be known. Additionally, electronic searching provides the ability to combine fields or terms (using Boolean logic, quotation marks, and so on). The obvious disadvantage of using electronic sources is the cost involved (hardware, software, connectivity time). This should be weighed against the advantages of speed and the currency of the information accessed.

School librarians should select all reference sources—including factbooks, directories, almanacs, yearbooks, and handbooks—such that they answer the information requests of students. These types of resources will vary greatly from library to library. Sources included in a school library collection should be based on the students and community served, the types of questions asked, and the number of questions posed in a particular subject area (curriculum needs). Another critical factor in the selection process is the geographic location of the school. This may dictate a concentration of sources dealing with a specific locality. The budget available must obviously be taken into account. Decisions about which of the specialized factbooks, directories, almanacs, yearbooks, and handbooks to purchase are not as easily made as the decision to buy general sources of these types. These reference tools offer a very good value at a low cost. However, school library media centers generally have smaller collections of this nature than public and larger academic libraries. The age and level of the student population affects the resources selected and the format. For example, elementary school libraries tend to have a larger print reference collection than middle school and high school libraries because young students have difficulty with Internet resources that are generally designed for an older audience. As with all reference resources, review journals—tools and aids—are available to assist with the proper and efficient evaluation and selection of factbooks, directories, almanacs, yearbooks, and handbooks.

Basic Sources

The factbooks, directories, almanacs, yearbooks, and handbooks discussed in this chapter include a sampling of the sources appropriate for school libraries. Actual selections will depend on your distinctive school situation. It should also be noted that these types of resources are not as plentiful (or used) in elementary levels as they are in secondary school library media centers.

FACTBOOKS

Factbooks are a very popular reference tool in school libraries because they are authoritative sources for answering basic questions students might pose and offer an excellent model to demonstrate how specific reference tools can be used for finding information. The *Guinness Book of Records*, published annually by Bantam, is probably the most famous factbook. It was first published in 1956 and is divided into chapters pertaining to specific subjects, such as the living world and human beings. *Guinness World Records* is now available online, as well (http://www.guinnessworld records.com/). There are many specific Guinness titles now published on a variety of topics, such as rock stars, names, and speed. *Famous First Facts*, published by H. W. Wilson, is another popular factbook for school library media centers. *Famous First Facts* is just that—an alphabetical subject list of first happenings, discoveries, and inventions in American history. An excellent factbook resource for school libraries is

Facts on File World News Digest Online covering political, social, cultural, and athletic events. Published by Infobase Publishing and updated twice weekly (factsonfile .infobasepublishing.com), this resource contains an archive of seven decades of news along with current events. It includes 200 biographies, more than 100 key events, overviews of 50 controversial issues, and thousands of hyperlinks. The resource is appropriate for middle school and high school students and is an excellent source for introducing young adults to people and events that have shaped and are shaping our world. The cost is reasonable for school libraries, and the scope of content is very broad. Specialized Facts on File titles covering specific subject areas are available in e-book and print formats. Excellent advertisement-supported Web sites for finding facts include *Information Please* (www.infoplease.com) and its associated children's site *FactMonster* (www.factmonster.com). Published by Pearson, a notable publisher of reference materials, these Web sites have the goal to provide reliable information, engage, and entertain.

An example of a statistical factbook often used in school libraries is the *Statistical Abstract of the United States*. This is a basic source of American statistical data, containing a collection of statistics on social and economic conditions in the United States as well as selected international data. *Statistical Abstract of the United States* is published annually and is available online (http://www.census.gov/compendia/ statab/) and in a printable PDF format. A factbook for countries of the world is available from the United States Central Intelligence Agency (CIA). The CIA World FactBook (https://www.cia.gov/library/publications/the-world-factbook/index.html) is a free information resource for facts about the history, people, government, economy, geography, communications, transportation, military, and global issues for over two hundred countries.

DIRECTORIES

Two obvious and well-used local directories are the telephone book and the city directory. Although offered separately in print format, they are available electronically (www.555–1212.com). The *National Directory of Addresses and Telephone Numbers* published biannually by Omnigraphics is another directory of this type. It contains more than 100,000 telephone numbers of businesses and government agencies across the United States. Additionally, fax numbers, addresses, zip codes, and toll-free numbers are provided. This directory is available in print and electronic formats. The *AT&T 800 Toll-Free Directory*, published irregularly by AT&T (1992 to present), includes AT&T residential and business toll-free numbers; it is free of charge. This directory is also available online (http://inter800.com). Also sponsored by AT&T, the *AnyWho Directory* is yet another useful directory for the location of telephone numbers and related data. By using the online *AnyWho Directory* (www.anywho.com), one can locate e-mail addresses, homepages, and toll-free numbers. This directory includes more than 90 million entries. *Americom Area Decoder* (http://decoder.americom.com/) is another online telephone directory. By entering a major city name, one can locate the area code, or by entering the area code, the major cities within that area can be found. Another directory site is www.internettollfree.com.

Literary Market Place, published annually by Information Today, is the ultimate directory (guide) to the U.S. book publishing industry. It includes more than 400,000 publishers and 12,000 firms that are directly or indirectly involved with book publishing in the United States, covering a multiplicity of aspects regarding the publishing business. *Literary Market Place* is available in print format (two volumes), and online (www.literarymarketplace.com). *BookWire* (www.bookwire.com), an online source regarding book-related sites (mentioned in chapter 3), is also a valuable resource for information regarding book publishing and related topics.

Numerous college and university directories exist that are extremely valuable for secondary school libraries. Two of the more well-known ones are *Peterson's College Database*, published annually by Peterson's (1987 to present) and available in an online version (www.petersons.com/college-search.aspx) and the *College Handbook*, published by the College Board (various dates) available in print format. Online directories are valuable resources when searching for college and university information. *College Net* (www.collegenet.com) claims to be the number one portal for applying to colleges worldwide. It includes more than 1,500 college and university online application forms. *All About College* (www.allaboutcollege.com) offers thousands of links to colleges and universities around the world, as well as admissions office e-mail addresses for most schools. Secondary students often request information about specific colleges and universities; these directories are very beneficial in answering questions of this nature.

The *Encyclopedia of Associations* is a directory published five times a year by Gale Research, which lists and describes more than 20,000 associations and organizations. Broad subjects with detailed indexes divide this directory; a typical entry covers 15 to 20 basic points about the association or organization. This is available in print format (three volumes) and as an e-book.

Directories are typically user-friendly reference tools. The scope is normally indicated in the title and the kind of information is limited and typically presented in an orderly, clear manner.

ALMANACS

Where a single figure or fact is required, the almanac can be very useful. Students enjoy facts and trivia; therefore, almanacs are wonderful sources for browsing as well as information seeking. The *World Almanac and Book of Facts*, published annually by Infobase Publishing (1868 to present, print format and via various online databases), provides brief, accurate essay pieces on topics of current interest. This almanac includes a quick reference index with approximately 80 broad subject headings; it also provides a section on maps and flags. *Time Almanac with Information Please* is yet another popular almanac for school library media centers available online and in print. The almanac features discursive, larger units on such subjects as the lively arts, science, education, and medicine. The makeup of this almanac is considerably more attractive, with larger type and spacing than the *World Almanac*. The *Time Almanac with Information Please* is also available online (www.infoplease.com). The *Daily Almanac* provides interesting facts about today's date. It includes categories such as Today's Figures, Today's Fun Facts, Today's Horoscope, Births, Deaths, and Special Events. The *Daily Almanac* is available online (http://www.infoplease.com/daily).

Multitudes of specialized almanacs are available; many of them suitable for school library media centers. The following are examples of almanacs of a specific nature. The *Almanac of American Politics* print version provides colorful profiles and insightful analysis of all members of Congress as well as governors. This almanac is arranged by state, name, and House committees. It is easily searchable and updated frequently. The online version is also available through the National Journal (http://www.nationaljournal.com/almanac/). The *Writer's Almanac*, available online (http://writersalmanac.publicradio.org/), can also be heard each day on public radio stations throughout the United States. This almanac is a daily program of poetry and history provided by Garrison Keillor. The *World Almanac of Presidential Quotations* (World Almanac) and the *World Almanac and Book of Facts* (World Almanac) are examples of the numerous useful almanacs for secondary school library media centers. The *Almanac of the 50 States* (Information Publications) is an example of an almanac particularly suitable for elementary school library media centers. Almanacs valuable for your specific school situation should be determined using appropriate selection and evaluation tools and aids, aligning them with the specific curriculum and information needs of your school population.

YEARBOOKS

Almost every imaginable area of human interest has its own yearbook. There are literally hundreds of yearbooks available. The following are some examples of yearbooks appropriate for school library media centers. The *Statesman's Yearbook*, published annually by Palgrave Macmillan, provides concise but complete descriptions of organizations and countries. It emphasizes the political and economic aspects of the world from 1864 to the present. The *American Book of Days*, published by H. W. Wilson and updated infrequently, discusses how and why holidays are celebrated. Beneath each day of the year this yearbook lists major and minor events, many of which are explained in detailed essays.

Common types of yearbooks, not to be overlooked for school library media centers, are encyclopedia yearbooks, published with most major encyclopedias. Encyclopedia yearbooks are resources that identify names, dates, statistics, events, and other important items of the preceding year. These yearbooks, however, are being published less often with the integration of electronic sources.

HANDBOOKS

Handbooks provide information about given fields of knowledge; they zero in on a specific area of interest. There are numerous handbooks and manuals, ranging from nature study to classical mythology. The handbooks purchased should be of value and interest to your school, community, and student population.

Masterplots II, published by Salem Press, is a popular handbook with secondary school students and is available in print and electronic formats. It provides plot summaries for more than 2,000 books and is a condensation of almost every important classic in the English language. *Monarch Notes*, available in print, electronic, and online formats, is published by the Bureau of Electronic Publishing. *Monarch Notes* is similar to *Masterplots II* and is useful for providing summaries of plot or content, character analyses, commentary on the texts, and author background data. Online sources using a handbook-style format include, for example, *Spark Notes* (www.sparknotes.com), which is extremely useful for students.

The *Occupational Outlook Handbook*, published biennially by the Government Printing Office, is also a well-used resource among secondary school students. This handbook, published by the U.S. Department of Labor, provides detailed descriptions of more than 300 occupations, covering 85 percent of all jobs in the United States. Each essay within *Occupational Outlook Handbook* indicates what a job is likely to offer in advancement, employment, location, earnings, and working conditions. The *Occupational Outlook Handbook* is also available online (http://www.bls.gov/oco/). A youth version is available on the BLS Kid's Page (http://www.bls.gov/k12/index.htm).

Bartlett's Familiar Quotations, published by Little, Brown, and Co. (print format), is by far the most famous book of quotations. This handbook, including more than 2,000 individuals and 20,000 quotations, is a collection of passages, phrases, and proverbs traced to their sources in ancient and modern times. Bartlett's (the older version) can also be found online (www.bartleby.com/100).

Facts on File publishes a number of different handbooks related to ancient civilizations of Greece, Rome, Mesopotamia, Egypt, Europe, and America. Recommended for high school libraries, these titles include thematic chapters, a detailed index, timelines, and photographs.

As previously mentioned, there are numerous handbooks covering an enormous range of topics. To engage students in the handbook format, the *Daring Book for Girls* and the *Dangerous Book for Boys* published by William Morrow, recall the nostalgic period when "how-to" books were published for boys and girls that contained a variety of hands-on projects and crafts. On a more academic note, the following are examples of handbooks, illustrating the wide variety available for school libraries today: *MLA Handbook for Writers of Research Papers* (Modern Language Association of America); *Publication Manual of the American Psychological Association* (American Psychological Association); *Mayo Clinic Family Health Book* (William Morrow); *Physicians' Desk Reference* (PDR Network); *21st Century Grammar Handbook* (Dell); *AIDS Crisis in America: A Reference Handbook* (ABC-CLIO); *Handbook of United States Coins* (Whitman); and *101 Creative Problem-Solving Techniques: The Handbook of New Ideas for Busine*ss (New Management Publishing Company).

There are countless factbooks, directories, almanacs, yearbooks, and handbooks. New ones, as well as old ones in new formats, including online and mobile applications, appear each year. It is obviously impossible to list all of them. In practice, as a school library media specialist, these reference sources should be selected primarily because they meet student's informational needs—but also because they portray the uniqueness of the school, student population, and community served.

Webliography

Bartlett's Familiar Quotations
> www.bartleby.com/100
> *This site offers more than 2,000 individuals and 20,000 quotations, phrases, and proverbs.*

The College Press Network
> www.thecollegepress.com
> *News information provided by young journalists. Information is organized by category.*

Consumer Reports
>   www.consumerreports.org/cro/index.htm
>   *ConsumerReport.org is fee-based. From this site, one can search automobiles, appliances, computers, health and fitness, personal finance, and more.*

Embarrassing Problems
>   www.embarrassingproblems.com
>   *Embarrassing Problems is a free Web site providing medical information about issues some would consider embarrassing.*

Fact Monster
>   www.factmonster.com/
>   *Published by Pearson, this is a one-stop general reference for the elementary age student.*

Facts on File World News Digest
>   www.factsonfile.infobasepublishing.com
>   *This online source offers accumulations of full-text articles from "News Digest."*

Fed Stats
>   www.fedstats.gov
>   *This site provides Links to Statistics and Links to Statistical Agencies—from over 100 U.S. federal agencies.*

Find Law
>   www.findlaw.com
>   *This Web site provides Legal News, For Legal Professionals, For Students, For the Public, For Businesses, and many other useful links.*

Food and Drug Administration
>   www.fda.gov/default.htm
>   *This site includes Products FDA Regulates, A–Z Index, Food Industry, Hot Topics, FDA Activities, and more.*

Guinness World Records
>   www.guinnessworldrecords.com/
>   *This online version offers a free newsletter; one can search areas such as Human Body, Amazing Feats, Natural World, Science and Technology, Arts and Media, and so on.*

Information Please
>   www.infoplease.com/
>   *Published by Pearson, this is an authoritative, one-stop, general reference for older students.*

Mayo Health Oasis
>   www.mayoclinic.com

This site includes areas such as Diseases and Conditions, Drug Search, Health Tools, Healthy Living, and Books and Newsletters (one newsletter is free).

The Monster Board
> www.monster.com
> *Via this Web site, one can apply for Online Jobs, Have Jobs E-mailed to You, Let A Company Find You, Search anywhere in the United States for a job, get career advice, and more.*

PDR Net
> www.pdr.net
> *This site is fee-based. It includes Drug Information, Medical References, Patient Education, Medical Marketplace, and much more.*

PubMed
> www.ncbi.nlm.nih.gov/entrez/query.fcgi?db=PubMed
> *This online site is fee-based and is offered by the National Library of Medicine. It includes more than 14 million citations for biomedical articles from MEDLINE and other life science journals.*

The Quotations Page
> www.quotationspage.com
> *The Quotations Page is an online catalog of quotation resources on the Internet.*

RefDesk
> www.refdesk.com
> *This Web site offers Search RefDesk, Search Dictionary, Search Thesaurus, In the News, Local News, Today in History, Current Events Topics, and more.*

Snopes
> www.snopes.com
> *This interesting site includes, for example, Urban Legends Reference page, Autos, Music, Luck, Business, Horrors, Humor, Holidays, and Military.*

DIRECTORIES

All About College
> www.allaboutcollege.com
> *This site offers thousands of links to colleges and universities, as well as admissions offices, e-mail addresses, and much more.*

Americom Area Decoder
> http://decoder.americom.com
> *This online telephone directory assists one in locating area codes, cities, and so forth.*

AnyWho Directory
> www.anywho.com
> *Via this online site, one can locate e-mail addresses, homepages, and toll-free numbers.*

AT&T 800 Toll-Free Directory
> http://www.corp.att.com/directory/
> *This Web site includes AT&T residential and business toll-free numbers—free of charge.*

Big Yellow
> www.superpages.com
> *This Web site provides maps, driving directions, global directories, and much more.*

BookWire
> www.bookwire.com
> *This Web site is an extremely valuable online source regarding book-related sites.*

College Net
> www.collegenet.com
> *This Web site claims to be the number one portal for applying to colleges over the Web—a very useful online source.*

Literary Market Place
> www.literarymarketplace.com
> *This notable Web site is a guide to the U.S. book publishing industry.*

People Finder
> www.peoplefinder.com
> *This Web site offers People Search, People Finder, Background Checks, and Court Records; it also locates "best finders and prices."*

Peterson's College Database
> www.petersons.com/
> *This online resource offers an inclusive list of colleges and universities.*

Standard & Poor's Register
> www.standardandpoors.com/home/en/us
> *This famous Web site is a provider of credit ratings and other financial products and services.*

Statistical Abstract of the United States
> www.census.gov/compendia/statab/
> *This Web site is a basic source of American statistical data—containing a collection of statistics about social and economic conditions in the United States and internationally.*

Telephone Book and City Directory
    www.555–1212.com
    This online source is a local directory, offering a telephone book and city directory.

Who Where?
    www.whowhere.com
    This site searches more than 100,000 databases and resources, including public records.

ALMANACS

Daily Almanac
    www.infoplease.com/daily
    This site provides interesting facts about today's date, such as Today's Figures, Today's Fun Facts, Today's Horoscope, Special Events, and so on.

Information Please Almanac
    www.infoplease.com/ almanacs.html
    This Web site features such subjects as arts, science, education, and medicine.

Information Please Kids Almanac
    http://www.factmonster.com/almanacs.html
    This online source is a kid-friendly version of Information Please.

The Old Farmer's Almanac
    www.almanac.com
    This Web site offers information about Astronomy, Weather, Gardening, Food, Press, Shop, Today in History, and more.

YEARBOOKS AND HANDBOOKS

Occupational Outlook Handbook
    www.bls.gov/oco/home.htm
    This site provides detailed descriptions of more than 300 occupations.

Chapter **5**

Biographical Sources

Introduction

People are interesting; learning about individuals is fascinating. Students learn about people because they are curious and want to discover what others are like and have accomplished. What do biographical sources do? What is their purpose? Biographies tell about what people have done or what they are doing, whether it is their occupations, dates of birth, major accomplishments, or their lives in general. They are sources of fact as well as pictures of everyday life. As explained by William A. Katz (2002), "In reference work, the primary use of biography is: 1) to locate people who are famous in a given occupation, career, or profession; 2) to locate supporting material about an individual for any number of reasons from a paper on the fall of Rome to a study on the modern automobile's brake system; and not the least, 3) to locate a possible name for a baby" (343).

Types of Biographical Sources

Two basic types of biographical sources are available: direct and indirect. Direct sources provide factual information about a person, such as date of birth, date of death, place of birth, career history, and so on. Well-known examples of direct sources are *Current Biography* and *Who's Who*. Indirect sources list bibliographic citations leading the student to other works that may contain the information sought. Typically these sources are indexes to other sources. *Biography Index* (EBSCO), *World Biography Index* (updated semiannually by Thomson Gale) and *Biography and Genealogy Master Index* (Gale Group) are examples of online indirect sources. These two types of biographical sources can be further divided into two categories: current and retrospective. Current sources provide information about living persons; retrospective sources supply information about historical figures. Some biographical tools give data on both living and dead individuals. Regardless of type or category, biographical sources vary in extent and coverage. Some sources, for example, focus on one profession or academic field, such as *American Presidents: Life Portraits*, which can be found online (www.americanpresidents.org) or *Contemporary Authors* (Gale Group). Another class of biographies includes prominent figures from all fields, such as *Marquis Who's Who* database (http://www.marquiswhoswho.com/). Biographical sources can also be international in scope such as *UXL Encyclopedia of World Biography* (Gale). The interest in the lives of others is universal; as a result, biographical sources are an essential and significant reference tool for school librarians.

Evaluation and Selection

Evaluation of Biographical Sources

COST
- Determine the most useful format in relation to your budget.
- Consider one-volume sources as opposed to full-volume sets.
- Always take into account the needs of the school and student population.

ACCURACY
- Note that primary resources may have items omitted.
- Also note that secondary resources may be incorrect or biased.

COMPREHENSIVENESS
- The criteria for inclusion should be included in the prefatory material.
- The scope and criteria should be in agreement.

EASE OF USE
- The source should be concise, organized, and straightforward.
- Indexes and cross references should be included.

CURRENCY
- Compare sources with other similar resources to determine if it is up-to-date.
- Check publisher frequency.

How does a school library media specialist know if a biographical source is legitimate, authoritative, and based on accurate material? One hint: the title should be listed in basic bibliographies, such as *Guide to Reference Books* and *American Reference Books Annual*. The publisher's name is another indication of authority. Four popular publishers of biographies are Gale Group, EBSCO, Macmillan/St. Martin's Press, and Reed Elsevier. As with all other reference sources for school library media centers, evaluation and selection of appropriate biographical items must be based on the needs of the school, students, and community. These sources vary widely according to age level, location of school, and numerous other variables. Students require biographies for research purposes, for general information needs, as well as to satisfy their personal curiosity. Both current and retrospective biographical sources are essential tools in library media centers.

Evaluation of Electronic Bibliographies

The following criteria should be considered when evaluating electronic bibliographies.

CONTENT
- A high percentage of the content should be full-text.
- Images should be used to enhance the content.
- Basic and advanced search features should be available.
- Scope statement should be available.

VENDOR
- Customer Service and Support should be offered through a help desk or phone support.
- Training should be provided for staff and students.

STATISTICAL
- Reports on usage should be easily exported or printed.
- Results of reports should be easily interpreted.
- Type of Reports may be determined by vendor or library.

TECHNICAL
- Authentication—is username and password set by vendor or school?
- Access—is user access limited to the school day or anytime?
- Proxy/Firewall—are there complications for configuring the network proxy/firewall?

An overriding factor regarding selection of biographical sources is cost. As a school library media specialist, you must consider the importance of purchasing full-volume sets or a concise one-volume source. You must also decide which format will be most useful in relation to the cost. Should the biographical source be print or purchased as an online resource? These issues must be weighed according to budget and needs of the student population. Does your library media center have the hardware to warrant the purchase of online services? Are the students capable of efficiently and effectively searching electronically? Many biographical sources are changing from print format to online searchable databases. Obviously, searching an electronic format is typically more thorough than searching a print source. In addition, one is able to scan thousands of possibilities in seconds, rather than laboriously searching individual indexes and sources. Electronic sources can also include video clips, links to other Web sites, and so forth, which are additional advantages. Your school, students, community, cost, and individuality of your library media center will all play a role in the effective selection of biographical sources. How does a school library media specialist know if a biographical source, print or electronic, is legitimate and accurate? As with other reference tools, biographical sources should be evaluated as to their accuracy, comprehensiveness, and ease of use. For current resources, the information must be as up-to-date as possible.

Of critical importance in evaluating a biographical source is the accuracy of the information provided. Basically, there are two sources of this information: the biographies themselves and information provided or written about individuals (secondary sources). While biographies are certainly capable of providing accurate information, authors may omit facts regarded as unfavorable. Retrospective biographical sources must rely on secondary sources for the information. These sources may have incorrect or biased information, depending on the author. To verify questionable information, consult other resources.

Typically, the criteria for inclusion in a specific biographical source are provided in prefatory material. However, how those criteria are defined and applied determines how comprehensive the source is. Attempt to locate as many individuals as possible who meet the criteria, as this increases the value of the resource. Often the criteria are stated in general terms and, hence, are difficult to determine. Regardless of the criteria used, the source's scope and criterion should be in agreement.

When evaluating biographical sources, as with all other reference tools, ease of use is a critical factor. If the source is poorly organized, or if the indexes or cross-references are inadequate, the information desired may never be located. Obviously, electronic sources offer a definite advantage over print materials concerning ease of use. Electronic retrieval allows students to retrieve biographical entries for individuals with common characteristics, such as date of birth, occupation, and so forth. Electronic searching also permits students to simultaneously search entries from numerous different printed editions or volumes of a specific biographical tool. Information, regardless of format, should be presented in a concise, organized, and straightforward fashion.

Currency is also an important factor when evaluating biographical sources. Out-of-date information can lead to inaccuracies regarding an individual's address, current profession, and so on. Comparing entries for the same person in varying biographical sources may assist in revealing errors. Publication frequency is another issue in maintaining current information about biographies. Biographical directories are typically revised every year or two. However, the electronic versions of these sources are often updated only when a new print edition is prepared; therefore, they may be no more current than the print sources.

In selecting and evaluating biographical sources, tools and aids are available to assist school librarians. Many of the review journals (as described in a previous chapter) contain separate sections regarding reference sources. These tools should be used to identify the most suitable biographical sources for your school situation. In addition, as with other reference resources, elicit the assistance of faculty members and experts in the field.

Dealing as much with individual ego and pride as with accomplishment and fact, early biographical reference sources were great sources of income for what some call the tin cup brigades. These were people who literally moved into a community, established a biographical book of that community, and then charged individuals for an entry. These mug books are a far cry from the legitimate works. Yet, ironically enough, historians are grateful for the information they provide of America. Even today, vanity biographical schemes abound.

Basic Sources

There are numerous biographical reference sources available on every imaginable significant person and in every format. The focus of this section, however, is biographical sources appropriate for use in school library media centers. The sources appropriate for your school library media center will depend on your situation—the school, students, and community, as well as budget and personal preferences. The biographical sources mentioned are commonly used; they are not all-inclusive, but merely examples that are suitable for school library media centers. Further information about specific biographical sources is presented in journals and other selection and evaluation tools.

Current Biographical Dictionaries

Biographical dictionaries are print and online compilations of biographies of notable persons, living or dead, in particular subject areas and arranged alphabetically. Many of the biographical dictionaries developed for the K–12 community are incorporated into electronic database packages offered by publishers such as EBSCO or Facts on File. The resources included here are merely highlights of the many biographical dictionaries available today.

Who's Who in America, available in print and online formats from Marquis Who's Who (http://www.marquiswhoswho.com/), is a current biographical dictionary that is a useful source for many school library media centers. The print version is arranged alphabetically and includes individuals for their achievements and contributions to society. Inclusion is not based simply on wealth or notoriety. The information about individuals is obtained from the biography, if possible. *Who's Who in America* is used primarily to locate basic information about individuals such as date of birth, positions held, address, degrees earned, and the like. Who's Who publishes four U.S. regional directories: East, Midwest, West, and South. Canada is included in each regional Who's Who. Illustrations of specialized Who's Who publications include *Who's Who in American Art* and *Who's Who in American Politics*. Who's Who is also international in scope. Two examples are *Who's Who in the World* and *Who's Who in Asia*. The online version is updated daily and contains the information from 24 Who's Who print titles with 1,444,914 biographies available.

Current Biography and the online version of *Current Biography Illustrated* (EBSCO, print format; published monthly; online; fee-based; http://www.ebscohost .com/academic/current-biography-illustrated) are two of the most recognized current biographical dictionaries. *Current Biography* provides objective and carefully researched biographical essays about persons in a wide range of fields who are prominent in their disciplines. The essays are primarily based on articles that have appeared in magazines and newspapers. Each essay includes a photograph of the subject and a list of sources upon which the essay is based. It provides a life history of the individual without reading a full biography. Each issue of *Current Biography* contains approximately 15 essays. The online version offers searching by name, profession, place of origin, gender, ethnicity, birth/death dates, titles of works, and key words for more than 25,000 articles and obituaries.

A widely used biographical source for middle and high schools is *Biography Today*. This source is published annually by Omnigraphics in three softbound issues and one bound, cumulative volume. Six regular subject series in politics, the arts, science, and sports are also available. Selected biographies are also available in Spanish. Each issue of *Biography Today* contains entries for approximately 10 people, judged to be of interest to young adults.

An extremely valuable online biographical source is bio. (http://www.biography .com). This resource offers more than 20,000 personalities and 2,400 videos for the user to search. The site also features Born on This Day, On This Day, Biographies on Arts and Entertainment, Features, and numerous other useful biographical elements.

Native American Biography Sources and Literary Criticism

<table>
<tr><th colspan="1">Print Resources</th></tr>
<tr><td>

- *American Indian Autobiography* (University of California Press) (November 1988)
- *American Indian Literature: An Anthology* (University of Oklahoma Press) (July 1991)
- *A Bibliography of Native American Writers 1772–1924* (Scarecrow Press) (September 1981)
- *Biographical Dictionary of Indians of the Americas* (American Indian Publishing) (February 2008)
- *Blue Dawn, Red Earth: New Native American Storytellers* (Doubleday)
- *Dictionary of Native American Literature* (Garland Publishing)
- *Harper's Anthology of 20th Century Native American Poetry* (Harper & Row)
- *Home Places: Contemporary Native American Writings* (University of Arizona Press)
- *Literature By and About the American Indian: An Annotated Bibliography* (Illinois National Council of Teachers of English)
- *Literature of the American Indian: Views and Interpretations. A Gathering of Indian Memories, Symbolic Contexts and Literary Criticism* (New American Libraries)
- *Native American Literature* (Twayne Publishers)
- *Native American Literature: A Brief Introduction and Anthology* (HarperCollins College Publishers)
- *Native American Women: A Biographical Dictionary* (Garland Publishing)
- *Native Americans Autobiography: An Anthology* (University of Wisconsin Press)
- *Native Americans: Portrait of the Peoples* (Visible Ink Press)
- *Returning the Gift: Poetry and Prose from the First North American Native Winter's Festival* (University of Arizona Press)
- *Who Was When in Native American History: Indians and Non-Indians from Early Contacts Through 1900* (Facts on File)

</td></tr>
</table>

Author sources is one significant area in many school media reference collections. Students study and learn about the lives of authors as a part of the curriculum. The library media center can supplement these studies with visiting authors and other similar activities. The following are examples of author sources appropriate for school library media centers. *Contemporary Authors*, published by Gale Reference Publishing (print format is updated annually; online format continuously), is a current biographical dictionary. This source includes not only authors of books, but also journalists, musicians, and more. Another similar biographical source is *Something About the Author* (Gale Reference Publishing; e-book and print formats). Several volumes are published each year, and each volume contains a cumulative index to the entire set, which includes authors and illustrators of works created for children and young adults. *World Authors*, part of EBSCO's Biography Reference Bank, is yet another well-known series on authors. This international source includes not only essential biographical information, but also bibliographies or works by and about the author. Entries are nearly 1,000 words, with a picture of the author and a listing of published works.

There are also numerous online sources regarding authors and literary criticism such as Special Collections at the Internet Public Library (www.ipl.org/div/special) and the Children's Literature Web Guide (www.people.ucalgary.ca/~dkbrown/). Online resources offer excellent author information as well as sections on literary criticism.

Retrospective Biographical Dictionaries

Retrospective biographical dictionaries differ from current dictionaries in that they typically include only individuals who are not living. A major biographical source of this type for school library media centers is the *Encyclopedia of World Biography* (Gale) composed of 17 volumes of text in the second edition. The e-book version contains all 17 volumes plus 18 annual supplement volumes. This source was compiled specifically for students in secondary schools. For ready-reference purposes the *Dictionary of American Biography* (Charles Scribner's Sons) is an excellent source for extensive biographical information about prominent deceased Americans. There are more than 18,000 entries, arranged alphabetically by surname. The entries, written by scholars, are entirely in essay format and vary from a couple of paragraphs to several pages (a few as long as 10 pages). Equally useful is the *American National Biography*, available online (www.anb.org/aboutanb.html). The *Concise Dictionary of American Biography* (Charles Scribner's Sons) is a one-volume work that provides brief entries for each individual. Some entries offer only basic facts, while more important figures have short essays about the individual. Another important retrospective source is *Marquis Who Was Who in America* (Marquis; print and online formats). This source provides basic factual data about deceased prominent Americans; it is revised every four to five years in print format and continuously online.

Indirect biographical sources tell where information about individuals may be found rather than providing the information directly. An indirect source is the best place to start a search for information about a person if the student requests a number of different sources. *Biography Index* (EBSCO) offers references to biographical articles in over a million article and book citations. This resource is available online as part of EBSCO's Biography Reference Bank.

Conclusion

School librarians have a massive number of biographical sources from which to choose. The purpose of this chapter is to introduce you to types of biographical sources and to provide useful examples within each type. Each school library media center will require different sources depending on the unique situation surrounding it. Not only are there a wide variety of biographical sources, both individual and collective, but resources now also come in a selection of formats as well. Additionally, it should not be overlooked that biographical information can be found in other reference sources, such as encyclopedias. The search strategy employed will depend on the type and amount of biographical information requested. As with the majority of reference questions, the first step is to obtain as much information as possible from the student. Can the question be answered by searching one source (ready-reference) or do a variety of sources need to be consulted (research)? Regardless of the question, it can only be answered if the proper biographical sources are available and correctly applied in your school library media center.

Webliography and Additional Examples of Online Biographical Resources

American Academy of Achievement
> http://www.achievement.org
> *This Web site provides biographies of high achievers in the arts, business, public service, science and exploration, sports, etc.*

American National Biography (ANB) Online
> http://www.anb.org/aboutanb.html
> *This site provides the latest update of the American National Biography Online, which comprises 24 volumes, including ones on recently deceased notables and intriguing figures from the 17th and 18th centuries.*

American Presidents: Life Portraits
> http://www.americanpresidents.org
> *This site contains a complete video archive of all American presidents: Life Portraits programming, plus these additional resources: Biographical Facts, Key Events of each presidency, Presidential Places, and Reference Material.*

bio.
> http://www.biography.com
> *This online resource searches more than 25,000 of the greatest lives—past and present.*

Biography Dictionary
> http://www.s9.com/
> *This site includes nearly 30,000 notable men and women who have shaped our world from ancient times to present day. One can search by name, year, profession, literary or artistic work, achievement, and much more.*

Children's Literature Web Guide
> http://people.ucalgary.ca/~dkbrown
> *This Web site includes Features, Discussion Boards, Quick Reference, and many more links (Authors on the Web, Stories on the Web, and so forth).*

Contemporary Literature—Authors Bios

    http://contemporarylit.about.com/od/authorprofiles/Author_Profiles.htm
    From Abbey to Yen Mah. From Le Carré to LeGuin. From Barry to Barry . . .
    there are thousands of authors to consider and new profiles added daily via
    this site.

Current Biography

    http://www.ebscohost.com/academic/current-biography-illustrated
    This Web site reflects the entire contents of the printed monthly Current
    Biography; it contains reliable information about people making tomorrow's
    headlines, plus historical figures back to World War II.

Dead People Server

    http://dpsinfo.com/dps/
    This is a database of interesting celebrities who are long dead or newly dead.
    (An unconventional site!)

Distinguished Women of the Past and Present

    http://www.distinguishedwomen.com
    This Web site offers biographies of women who contributed to their fields
    in different ways, including writers, educators, scientists, heads of state,
    politicians, artists, entertainers, and so on.

Infoplease.com/People

    http://www.infoplease.com/people.html
    The Infoplease biography search page contains data from the Columbia
    Encyclopedia, the Infoplease Dictionary, and Information Please Almanac—
    extremely useful!

Lives, The Biography Resource

    http://www.amillionlives.net/
    This site is the largest guide to post-human biography on the Web (people who
    have died); it provides links to biographies, autobiographies, memoirs, diaries,
    letters, narratives, oral histories, and resources on biographical criticism and
    special collections.

Reference Center at the Internet Public Library

    http://www.ipl.org
    This site provides the biographies section of IPL—including such subheadings
    as Artists and Architects, Authors, Entertainers, Musicians and Composers,
    Politicians and Rulers, and Scientists and Inventors.

Thinkers 50

    http://www.thinkers50.com
    This Web site ranks the top 50 business thinkers of all time and includes
    biographical information.

Chapter 6

Dictionaries and Encyclopedias

One might ask, "Do dictionaries and encyclopedias still matter today?" You bet! More dictionaries and encyclopedias are available—in an amazing range of topics, print and nonprint—than ever before! Remember that there is such a thing as an intellectual division of labor—not only among people, but also among types of books and reference materials. Sometimes a dictionary or encyclopedia is precisely what is required, regardless of format. How fortunate our students are to have access to thousands of dictionaries and encyclopedias, to meet the needs of every student in every imaginable situation.

Dictionaries indicate spelling, meaning, pronunciation, and syllabication of words. General encyclopedias capsulate and organize the world's accumulated knowledge. This chapter discusses types of dictionaries and encyclopedias appropriate for school library media situations (print, electronic, and online), as well as selection and evaluation of these vital reference sources.

DICTIONARIES

Introduction

Dictionaries are primarily thought of as a means of verifying spelling and defining words. Dictionaries are of two basic types and can be defined as: 1) a reference resource containing words systematically arranged along with information about their forms, pronunciations, functions, etymologies, meanings, and syntactical and idiomatic uses; and 2) a reference source alphabetically listing terms or names important to a particular subject or activity, along with discussion of their meanings and applications. Dictionaries may either be descriptive (how the language is actually used) or prescriptive (how it ought to be used). The descriptive philosophy claims that language is ever changing and that dictionaries should reflect those changes. Believers of the descriptive viewpoint realize that few rules are absolute; different societal and cultural situations offer their own rules. The prescriptive view claims that the major role of dictionaries is to set standards, support traditional usage, and prevent corruption of language by jargon and slang. Most of the Merriam-Webster dictionaries take the stance that "almost anything goes" as long as it is popular. For example, did you know that "ASAP" is currently a real word in the dictionary? At the other end of the spectrum are dictionaries that provide absolute rules of usage, such as *Webster's New World Dictionary*. Somewhere between descriptive and prescriptive dictionaries are the more practical types, such as the *American Heritage Dictionary*.

Two categories of dictionaries are unabridged and abridged. An unabridged dictionary attempts to include all of the words in the language that are in use at the time the dictionary is assembled. Unabridged dictionaries contain more than 265,000 words. Abridged dictionaries are selectively compiled and typically based on a larger dictionary. They are created for a certain level of student use. Most dictionaries are abridged. Types of dictionaries other than English language include foreign language, historical, geographical, biographical, slang and dialect, reverse dictionaries, thesauri, subject, visual, and so forth.

Evaluation and Selection

Evaluation of Dictionaries

AUTHORITY
- A reputable publisher is important (print and electronic).
- Examples of reputable publishers include:

Merriam-Webster	Macmillan
Random House	Simon & Schuster
Scott Foresman/Pearson	Oxford University Press
Houghton Mifflin Harcourt	

FORMAT
- Consider binding, arrangement of words, and readability.
- Note the effectiveness of purpose as stated in the title or introduction.
- Dictionaries in electronic format should have consistent display of information and navigation along with simple and advanced search functions.

CURRENCY
- Dictionary revision is never ending; a major advantage of electronic dictionaries is rapid update.

ACCURACY
- Spelling and definition should be precise.
- Words should be modernized.
- Meanings should be precise and clearly indicated.
- Definitions should be understandable and unambiguous.

Remember, above all else, that no dictionary is perfect; language is continually evolving (remember "ASAP"?). Each dictionary has its good features and its defects. Basically, dictionaries are written for a specific audience, such as high school students, or for a particular purpose. In evaluating dictionaries, it is critical to determine the degree to which a dictionary has succeeded in fulfilling the purpose of the population addressed. These are exceptionally critical elements for school librarians, as unique populations are served via dictionaries. The following criteria should be considered when evaluating dictionaries for school library media centers: authority, format, currency, and accuracy.

The authority or reputation of the publisher is an essential factor in judging the quality of dictionaries because staffs, rather than individuals, normally compile them. As with other reference areas, there are reputable publishers for general dictionaries, as well. The larger, better-known publishers in North America include Merriam-Webster, Random House, Scott Foresman/Pearson, Houghton Mifflin Harcourt, Macmillan, Simon and Schuster, and Oxford University Press. Additional reputable publishers exist for specialized dictionaries. Reputation of the publisher remains a vital factor in electronic versions as well. The same publishers as the print versions create many electronic dictionaries. The authority of online dictionaries is important to establish. Some online dictionaries, such as *Wiktionary*, use the social media model for developing and maintaining the contents. This means that anyone can create or edit an entry, and there is no single authority monitoring the site. For this reason, among others, it is wise to use selection tools such as *Choice Reviews* or *School Library Journal* for choosing the online dictionaries used in a school library.

Major format considerations for dictionaries include binding, arrangement of words, and readability. Even in today's electronic environment, school libraries should have a minimum of one print unabridged, hardcover dictionary that will withstand frequent use. Readability is a particularly important consideration for school library media centers. Is the print size large enough; is boldface type used effectively; is it clear and user-friendly? Dictionaries should be judged on their effectiveness of purpose as stated in the title, purpose, or introduction, regardless of format. For example, an elementary-level dictionary should include words likely to be used in reading and writing by an elementary student. The major advantages of dictionaries in electronic format are multiple access points and time saved by searching, as well as the numerous types offered via the Internet. When a dictionary is Web-based, a school librarian should ask all of the customary questions regarding its relative value to a printed version. It is also important, however, to consider other variables that relate to Internet resources, such as graphics, links, maneuverability, and so on.

Currency is yet another important factor to consider when evaluating dictionaries. Dictionary revision is never-ending. New words, revised definitions of older words with new meanings, and deletions and additions of technical and popular terms are continually occurring. An obvious advantage of Web-based dictionaries is rapid updates. Be aware, however, that just because a dictionary is on the Internet does not necessarily mean that it is authoritative or more current than the print equivalent.

In determining the accuracy of dictionaries, two basic considerations are spelling and definition. Where there are several forms of spelling, they should be clearly indicated. Frequently, two different spellings are provided, and both are acceptable. One should check words that have been modernized. Dictionaries typically provide the modern meaning of words first. Meanings should be precise, separate, and distinct, as well as clearly indicated. Definitions should reflect the meaning(s) of words in understandable, unambiguous terms. Illustrative examples or quotations from literature can assist in defining words in context.

The selection of dictionaries, as well as other reference materials, should be based on the particular needs and requirements of the school, student population, and community served. Additional elements to consider include the age and condition of print dictionaries currently in the school media center collection, along with budget. The long, useful life of a large, unabridged print dictionary will typically justify the cost. Become aware, however, of the plethora of wide-ranging dictionaries available via the Internet. Also, remain alert to dictionaries geared specifically for school libraries. It should be noted that college-level dictionaries might be valuable in high school library media centers, particularly for advanced students. One little-known, generally misunderstood belief is that there is no copyright on the use of the word *Webster*; this word is common property and can be used by any publisher. When selecting dictionaries, it is advisable to read reviews and stick with standard titles or publishers. Often titles will be available in print or e-book formats. Several selection tools are available for dictionaries, such as reviews provided in *Booklist* or *School Library Journal*.

Basic Sources

ENGLISH LANGUAGE DICTIONARIES

Probably the most notable unabridged dictionary of the English language is *Webster's Third New International Dictionary of the English Language* (Merriam-Webster). This large, comprehensive dictionary includes such items as the date when a word or phrase first entered the language and identification of vocabulary specifically of the American origin. Random House offers an unabridged dictionary in print format, entitled the *Random House Webster's Unabridged Dictionary*. This current, descriptive-style dictionary includes more than 300,000 entries and 2,500 illustrations.

Numerous abridged dictionaries exist that are appropriate for school library media centers. *Merriam-Webster's Collegiate Dictionary* (print, online, CD-ROM formats) represents an extensive revision and updating in both the entries and special sections. Each entry includes the part of speech, pronunciation, inflections, etymology, definitions, and notes on usage and synonymy. Definitions in this dictionary are precise and clear. Another useful abridged dictionary in print and electronic format is the *American Heritage Concise Dictionary*, which is the abridged version of the *American Heritage Dictionary of the English Language, Fourth Edition* (Houghton Mifflin Harcourt). This dictionary is particularly appropriate for high school students. It is easy to read, and the typeface and illustrations are large and clear. The *American Heritage Concise Dictionary* is extremely complete for a condensed edition. Other suitable abridged dictionaries in print format are *Webster's New World Dictionary of American English* and *Merriam-Webster's Collegiate Dictionary* (Merriam-Webster).

Print materials are used most often in the elementary grades because young children often experience difficulties with managing the more adult-oriented online environment. For primary and elementary age students, the following abridged dictionaries in print format are appropriate: *American Heritage Children's Dictionary*,

American Heritage First Dictionary, and *American Heritage Picture Dictionary* (Houghton Mifflin Harcourt); *Macmillan First Dictionary* (Simon & Schuster); *Longman Elementary Dictionary* (Pearson Longman); *Merriam-Webster's Elementary Dictionary* (Merriam-Webster); *Thorndike-Barnhart Children's Dictionary* (Addison Wesley); *DK First Dictionary* (Dorling Kindersley); and *Webster's New World Children's Dictionary* (Wiley). I am particularly fond of the following dictionaries mentioned above: *Thorndike-Barnhart Children's Dictionary* provides information regarding how to use the dictionary, as well as synonym studies and word source sections. It includes more than 25,000 words, 800 study pages, and more than 1,000 color photographs and other artwork. *Webster's New World Children's Dictionary* offers colorful illustrations, as well as a comprehensive thesaurus and reference section. The *American Heritage Children's Dictionary* is approximately 1,000 pages in length and features a thesaurus, a section on phonics and spelling, as well as a reference section, synonyms, building vocabulary, and world histories.

There are a wide number of dictionaries available online through electronic licensing. Houghton Mifflin Harcourt offers the *American Heritage First Dictionary*, *American Heritage Student Dictionary*, *American Heritage Children's Dictionary*, and *American Heritage College Dictionary* in electronic format. Free advertising-supported online dictionaries also exist from publishers of print dictionaries such as Macmillan (http://www.macmillandictionary.com) and Merriam-Webster (http://www .merriam-webster.com). Other online dictionaries suitable for school libraries include *Your Dictionary.com* (www.yourdictionary.com); *OneLook* (www.onelook.com); *Cambridge Dictionaries Online* (http://dictionary.cambridge.org); *Dictionary.com* (http://dictionary.reference.com); *Wordsmyth* (www.wordsmyth.net); Infoplease (http:// dictionary.infoplease.com); and *Oxford Dictionaries* (http://oxforddictionaries.com). Don't overlook these free resources!

FOREIGN LANGUAGE DICTIONARIES

A student who simply seeks a common foreign word or phrase is likely to find the answer in almost any general dictionary or in a reference such as *Browser's Dictionary of Foreign Words and Phrases* (Wiley). However, when it comes to more complicated, specialized words, students should refer to a bilingual dictionary or a bilingual visual dictionary. There are several reputable publishers of world language dictionaries in print and electronic format including Cassell/Wiley, HarperCollins, Charles Scribner's Sons/Gale, Simon & Schuster, Larousse, and Oxford University Press. These dictionaries all provide similar information, including pronunciations, definitions, slang words, colloquialisms, and idioms. Visual and picture world language dictionaries provide photos and illustrations so that students can make visual associations with the words. Examples of world language bilingual and visual dictionaries suitable for a school library include *Basic Japanese-English Dictionary* (Oxford University Press); *Children's Illustrated* bilingual dictionaries in Arabic, German, Italian, Russian, and Spanish (Hippocrene Books); *Firefly Five Language Visual Dictionary* (Firefly Books); and *Larousse College Dictionaries* in French and Spanish for high school language classes. Foreign language dictionaries are essential resources for school libraries. The types and number of foreign language dictionaries purchased will, of course, depend on the school's curriculum and student body. Schools with large numbers of second language learners should have picture dictionaries in different languages. Examples of dictionaries developed specifically for English language learners include *Let's Learn English Picture Dictionary* (McGraw-Hill), *Heinle Picture Dictionary* (Thomson Heinle), and the *American Heritage Dictionary for Learners of English* (Houghton Mifflin Harcourt). A number of publishers have made their collection of language dictionaries available online through subscription. *Oxford Language Dictionaries Online* (www.oxfordlanguagedictionaries.com) is an example of this type of resource. Examples of free online foreign language sources include *Word2Word.com* (www .word2word.com/dictionary.html); *Dictionaries by Language* (http://dir.yahoo.com/ Reference/Dictionaries/Language); *Your Free Language Wizard* (www.foreignword .com); *iLoveLanguages* (www.ilovelanguages.com); and *Glossaries by Languages* (www.lai.com/glossaries.html).

HISTORICAL DICTIONARIES

The *Oxford English Dictionary* (Oxford University Press, second edition), print and electronic formats, is a scholarly compilation (print is 22 volumes) including extensive etymologies that record the history of words and meanings in use since 1150. The purpose of this dictionary is to trace the history of the English language. The *Oxford English Dictionary* in electronic format (fee-based) contains definitions for most of the words in the English language and, in addition, information regarding their origins and quotations showing their range of meanings from the time they entered the language to present. The *New Shorter Oxford English Dictionary* (print format) is a current, two-volume historical dictionary. This dictionary includes more than 500,000 words and 80,000 quotations. The *New Shorter* is moderately priced and an excellent resource for etymologies and learning the fine points of history. The single volume *Barnhart Dictionary of Etymology* (H. W. Wilson) is yet another historical dictionary. An excellent feature of this dictionary is that it emphasizes the way language is written and spoken in the United States today. There are a number of etymological dictionaries online including *Dictionary.com* (http://dictionary.reference.com/etymology/) and *Online Etymological Dictionary* (http://www.etymonline.com/).

SLANG AND DIALECT DICTIONARIES

Does a school library need dictionaries on slang and dialect? This question is debatable and depends on the particular school and community served. However, slang and dialect dictionaries are useful for indicating the variations of meaning given slang words as well as providing expressions that are not well defined in an ordinary dictionary. The most notable slang and dialect dictionaries include: the *Oxford Dictionary of Modern Slang* (Oxford University Press); *Random House Historical Dictionary of American Slang* (Random House); and *Dictionary of American Regional English* (Harvard University Press). There are many slang dictionaries available online. One example is A Dictionary of Slang (http://www.peevish.co.uk/slang). Always be cautious regarding the nature of the language when allowing young children to use slang dictionaries.

THESAURI

A thesaurus is a specialized dictionary that deals solely with word synonyms and antonyms. The best-known thesauri are based on the work of Peter Mark Roget. It should be noted, as with the word "Webster's," "Roget's" cannot be copyrighted and is free to any publisher. The most notable Roget's thesaurus is the *Roget's International Thesaurus* (HarperCollins, print format). Two additional Roget's print formats that are valuable for school library media center collections are *Roget's A to Z* and *Roget's II: The New Thesaurus* (Houghton Mifflin). A thesaurus suitable for primary grades is the richly illustrated *Barron's First Thesaurus* (Barron's Educational Series). Many popular thesauri are available on CD-ROM and often integrated into common word processing programs. For example, *Merriam-Webster's Collegiate Thesaurus* is in CD-ROM and in PC download formats. Thesauri are also available online through electronic licensing and include *Roget's II: New Thesaurus*, *American Heritage® Children's Thesaurus*, and *American Heritage® Student Thesaurus* (Houghton Mifflin).Thesauri in electronic format have the advantage of rapid, easy searching, are often paired with dictionaries, and contain thousands of entries. Merriam-Webster's online Web site is a good example of how dictionaries and thesauri are combined as a single reference source (http://www.merriam-webster.com/) and make searching for the appropriate word or meaning a simple task for students.

SPECIALTY DICTIONARIES

Specialty dictionaries explain meanings of specific words in terms of professions, occupations, or areas of interest. When selecting specialty dictionaries, it is important to determine that there is no other resource currently in the collection that provides the same or remarkably similar information. One should look for purposeful illustrations, clear and thorough definitions, and current terminology in specialty dictionaries. There is an enormity of specialty dictionaries available dealing with every imaginable area of interest. The following resources are examples of the wide variety of specialty dictionaries available in print format that are appropriate for school libraries: *Dictionary of Classical Mythology* (Cassell Academic); *Harvard Dictionary of Music* (Belknap Press); *Dictionary of Media Terms* (Fitzroy Dearborn Publishing); *Dictionary of Geography* (Oxford University Press); *Dictionary of Science and Technology* (Academic Press); *Consumer's Dictionary of Food Additives* (Three Rivers Press); *Dictionary of Fictional Characters* (Writer Publishing); *Concise Dictionary of the Opera* (Oxford University Press); *Civil War Dictionary* (Vintage Books/Random House); and *New Dictionary of American Family Names* (New American Library). Topics of specialty dictionaries range from Accounting to Wine, and everything in-between. Two examples of online specialty dictionaries are A Basic Dictionary of ASL (American Sign Language) Terms (http://www.masterstech-home.com/asldict.html) and Strange and Unusual References (www.oneletterwords.com).

With dictionaries now available on most word processing software, the focus of general dictionaries has altered. Many features common to general dictionaries are an integrated part of word processing programs (spelling, synonyms, etc.). These elements provide easy and rapid access to basic dictionary functions. However, dictionaries offer much more than the basic word processing features. They provide an easy to navigate portal to new words and their meanings. As specialized terminology is not always included in general dictionaries integrated into word processing programs, subject specific dictionaries are a necessity. In addition, for language learners dictionaries are very useful to keep on hand to be consulted for new words and meanings. Finally, a dictionary is often required when one is not working at a computer. Therefore, there still remains a distinct and important place for numerous versions of general, foreign

Sample Specialty Dictionaries

American Heritage Children's Science Dictionary (Houghton Mifflin Harcourt)
This elementary-level resource includes over 2,500 entries in alphabetical order, with illustrations, tables, and charts.

Brave New Words: The Oxford Dictionary of Science Fiction (Oxford University Press)
A dictionary of over 1,000 terms used in science fiction books, TV, magazines, and movies is a popular addition to a high school reference collection.

Descriptionary (Facts on File)
A reverse dictionary for secondary collections that helps students find words and their meanings by broad categories.

Dictionary of the Global Economy (Franklin Watts/Scholastic)
Available in print and e-book formats, the resource for middle and secondary students includes over 400 entries on the topic of globalization, with colorful photos, charts, and sidebars.

Facts on File Specialized Dictionaries (Facts on File)
Facts on File offers a number of specialized dictionaries on the topics of science, computers and technology, music, language, and mythology.

Holidays, Festivals, and Celebrations of the World Dictionary (Omnigraphics)
Lists alphabetically thousands of special days around the world and includes indexes by chronology and subject.

Merriam-Webster's Geographical Dictionary (Merriam-Webster)
A comprehensive list of place-names with more than 250 maps and 130 tables.

Shakespeare's Language: A Glossary of Unfamiliar Words in His Plays and Poems (Facts on File)
The resource lists over 17,000 definitions to references, allusions, and expressions found in Shakespeare's plays.

Ultimate Visual Dictionary of Science (Dorling Kindersley)
Over 15,000 terms and 1,600 illustrations arranged by topic with a glossary of terms.

language, historical, slang and dialect, thesauri, and specialty dictionaries in today's modern, technological school libraries.

Webliography

A Basic Dictionary of ASL (American Sign Language) Terms
www.masterstech-home.com/ASLDict.html

*This site offers both animated and text definitions. The text definitions also
include letter or number sign images to aid in visualizing the sign.*

AskOxford

http://oxforddictionaries.com
*This Web site includes such features as Ask the Experts, Better Writing, World of
Words, Word of the Day, Quote of the Day, and much more.*

Cambridge Dictionaries Online

www.dictionary.cambridge.org
*This online dictionary ranges from intermediate to proficient level; it is clear,
up-to-date, and easy to use.*

Dictionaries by Language

http://dir.yahoo.com/Reference/Dictionaries/Language
This Web site includes everything from American Sign Language to Yiddish!

Dictionaries of Slang

http://www.peevish.co.uk/slang/
http://www.slangvocabulary.com/
http://onlineslangdictionary.com
These are online dictionaries of slang, with new slang added every month!

Dictionary.com

http://dictionary.reference.com
*This site includes such features as Bookstore, Fun and Games, Language
Resources, Thesurus.com, Tools, Translation, and Word of the Day.*

Glossaries by Languages

www.lai.com/glmain.html
*This is an extremely comprehensive site, including languages from Arabic to
Gaelic to Welsh.*

iLoveLanguages

www.ilovelanguages.com
*This Web site is a comprehensive catalog of language-related Internet resources.
The more than 2,000 links at iLoveLanguages have been hand reviewed.*

iTools

www.itools.com/lang/
*Via this site, one can learn the meaning of any word, its correct spelling, how to
pronounce it, and where it originated.*

Medline Plus

www.nlm.nih.gov/medlineplus/mplusdictionary.html
*This Web site is a gold mine of good health information from the world's largest
medical library, the National Library of Medicine.*

Merriam-Webster Online
    http://www.merriam-webster.com/
    This online source includes Merriam-Webster's Real Time Words, which consist of unedited entries randomly selected from millions of searches on Merriam-Webster Online that make the Top Ten List of the most frequently looked-up words.

OneLook
    www.onelook.com
    This Web site offers 6,002,182 words in 966 dictionaries, indexed!

Strange and Unusual References
    www.oneletterwords.com
    This site offers unusual dictionaries, such as the White Queen's Dictionary of One-Letter Words, Dictionary of All-Consonant Words, and Dictionary of All-Vowel Words.

Thesauri
    http://dmoz.org/Reference/Thesauri
    This site is the largest, most comprehensive human-edited directory on the Web. It is constructed and maintained by a vast, global community of volunteer editors.

Wiktionary
    http://www.wiktionary.org/
    A multilanguage online dictionary maintained by users as part of the Wikimedia Foundation effort to develop and distribute free multilingual content.

Wordsmyth
    www.wordsmyth.net
    This online source provides useful, accessible reference resources and is made expressly for elementary-school-aged children.

Word2Word.com
    www.word2word.com/dictionary.html
    This site provides links in the hope of developing a better understanding of others through the use of language; it offers numerous online dictionaries.

Your Dictionary.com
    www.yourdictionary.com
    This Web site uses the database of the American Heritage® Dictionary of the English Language(AHD), published by Houghton-Mifflin Company, as well as Roget's Thesaurus.

ENCYCLOPEDIAS

Introduction

"Do encyclopedias still matter? As school librarians, we believe that diversity in format, as well as in content, is vital to the reference collection. The ideal library [should] have numerous encyclopedias in many formats" (Quinn, 253).

Yes, encyclopedias have traveled remarkable distances over the past several decades with the expansion of new technologies. In all formats, encyclopedias remain essential reference sources for school libraries. A majority of ready-reference as well as research questions (to a degree), can be answered using encyclopedias, in all formats. The literal definition of an encyclopedia is a work that contains information on all branches of knowledge or comprehensively treats a particular aspect of knowledge, usually via articles arranged alphabetically by subject. The purposes of encyclopedias are to educate and inform. The Greek phrase for "encyclopedia" is *enkukliospaideia*, made up of *enkuklios*—"cyclical, periodic, ordinary" and *paideia*—"general education." These reference sources are unique in that they are organized and packaged in such a way that information is easily accessible and retrievable by the user. Encyclopedia compilers gather information from a variety of fields or from a single subject area and arrange them for rapid answers. Through detailed articles and brief facts, encyclopedias include a wide range of information on a multitude of topics. Note, however, that there are limitations on the breadth and depth of information contained in encyclopedias. These resources are useful for ready-reference, factual-type questions ("Where is Djibouti?"), to background information questions ("How is oil refined?"), to pre-research information (teaching systematic approaches to gathering information and becoming aware of larger issues and related concepts).

Encyclopedias should not be considered as sole sources of information, although they do assist in directing and strengthening a student's subsequent work. Encyclopedias still remain among the most frequently used reference materials in school library media centers (print and electronic). Differences in quality of print encyclopedias are subtle, but are a significant issue in online formats. In some cases, online encyclopedias like Wikipedia are created by volunteers who submit entries that are not always vetted by experts. In addition to the traditional print multivolume general encyclopedias, there are two other important types for school library media centers—single volume and subject encyclopedias. Encyclopedias can also be divided into three general categories: format (general, single volume, and subject); scope (general and subject); and audience (children, young adult, and layperson). Remain aware that encyclopedias are not proper resources for involved research; they are merely springboards to additional information.

Evaluating encyclopedias should be relatively simple. It is rare to discover errors in encyclopedia sets, since editorial standards are high in encyclopedia publishing. However, with some sets, there are problems with currency. Outdated material persists, not because the editorial staff is unaware of changes that should be made, but because the budget they are provided to work with merely allows them to update a certain number of pages each year. The cost of writing new copy is not the problem; indeed, some encyclopedias have updated articles in electronic formats that are not in the print set. It is production costs—setting type, making film, stripping in art or text—that limit the amount of revision in a print set of encyclopedias. Remember, however, that an encyclopedia is not expected to take the place of a newspaper in reporting current events. Other reference resources should be used to accomplish that. Keep in mind that bibliographies in encyclopedias should also be evaluated, noting the publication dates of materials listed. However, it is not necessarily a flaw to possess an old book in some subject areas, such as history.

Evaluation and Selection

Brief Evaluation of Encyclopedias

ACCURACY
- Look for standard titles.
- Consult appropriate review sources.

AUTHORITY
- Authority is determined by the scholars who write the articles or the publisher who distributes it.
- Look for prominent contributors.
- Stick with reputable publishing companies.

CURRENCY
- Edition does not indicate currency.

FORMAT
- Illustrations should be current, functional, clear, easy to follow, and appropriate for the intended audience.
- Layout, navigation links, motion, and sound in electronic formats should be functional, clear, and suitable for the audience.
- The source should be user friendly.
- The format should not interfere with the purpose.

INDEXING
- A detailed index is an absolute necessity for encyclopedias.
- Keyword and advanced search features should be a part of electronic formats.

OBJECTIVITY
- Do not assume objectivity.
- Check for passive or implicit biases.
- Notice what is excluded, emphasized, and deemphasized.
- Evaluate the advertising and potential biases on sponsored sites.

SCOPE
- The scope should be appropriate for the age group it claims to serve.
- The subject coverage should be uniform from discipline to discipline.
- Contemporary issues should be included.

Like dictionaries, encyclopedias are typically published with a specific audience in mind. The following criteria should be used when evaluating encyclopedias for school library use: accuracy, authority, currency, format, indexing, objectivity, and scope.

Accuracy and reliability of encyclopedias cannot be assumed. They, as all other reference sources, are written by individuals and, therefore, may inevitably contain errors. For evaluation purposes, one should look for standard titles and consult appropriate review sources. This applies to electronic as well as print versions.

Scholars who write or sign individual articles (or who are listed as contributors) and the publisher who distributes the encyclopedia determine the authority of encyclopedias. An editorial staff works; hence, even the scholars are limited by editorial parameters. In evaluating encyclopedias, one should look for prominent contributors, leaders in particular fields, and how their qualifications relate to the articles they wrote. It is also advisable to stick with reputable publishing companies. This remains true for electronic and Web-based encyclopedias, as well.

Currency of encyclopedias is not as much of a concern as it was in the past. Technologies have made the process of revising and updating considerably easier. Most large publishers claim to revise approximately 10 percent of print material in encyclopedias each year. This claim to ongoing revision is a major selling point, as publishers believe that no school library media center will purchase a new encyclopedia unless major revisions and updates have been made. Often the text will be revised while the bibliography remains dated. Be aware that the use of the word *edition* does not indicate currency. A printing of an encyclopedia is typically done at least once a year; electronic updates are provided more frequently.

Format is a vital element in evaluating encyclopedias for school library media centers. With the evolution of electronic and online encyclopedias, the criteria have altered somewhat; however, many of the same issues should be considered as for print encyclopedias. Are the illustrations (charts and maps) current, functional, clear, easy to follow, and appropriate for the intended audience? Is the motion and sound (electronic or Web-based formats) functional, clear, and suitable for the intended users? Does the motion and sound enhance the text or are they merely fun? Do the layout and navigation links make the resource user friendly with regard to locating information quickly and easily? The format of an encyclopedia should not interfere with the purpose. Evaluation of format for school librarians is largely dependent on understanding the product in terms of its appropriateness for the needs and characteristics of the school, student population, and community served.

A detailed index is an absolute necessity. Indexing (aka key word and advanced searching in online formats) is a means by which the user can be directed to the fullest range of information. Some children's print encyclopedias enhance accessibility with the inclusion of an index at the end of each volume, which refers to pages within the volume, as well as to related information in other volumes.

Many people believe that all encyclopedias are objective. This is not the case. One should check for objectivity and biases (particularly with online encyclopedias supported by advertising). Are both sides of a controversial issue represented? Be alert to passive or implicit biases as well, such as stereotyping. Notice what is excluded, emphasized, and deemphasized. Look at the size of one article as opposed to another. Remember that encyclopedias are published as a profit venture, one way or another.

Usually the scope of encyclopedias makes them ideal for reference work. The purpose is defined in terms of audience (age level) and emphasis (content and the way the content is presented). Who is the encyclopedia really for? Is it truly appropriate for the age group it claims to serve? It is extremely difficult for an encyclopedia to be equally useful for children and adults. Currently, emphasis is essentially a matter of deciding what compromise will be made between scholarship and popularity. Subject coverage should be uniform from discipline to discipline. Proportional length and depth of subjects should be checked, as well as the inclusion of contemporary issues.

The selection of encyclopedias appropriate for a school library will depend on the needs and requirements of the students served, as well as budget. Typically, encyclopedias provide information that is relatively general, clearly written, and free of jargon and complicated technical terminology. Generally speaking, library media centers have a great need for all types of encyclopedias and in all formats. Selection tools should be used to determine the most suitable encyclopedias for your situation. A basic selection tool is "Reference Books Bulletin" in the *Booklist* (American Library Association) journal. These reviews provide on a periodic basis detailed and timely information regarding encyclopedias.

Cost is another crucial factor in selecting appropriate encyclopedias. Although costs vary, purchasing print and e-book formats of encyclopedias is similar in that one typically purchases ownership, unlimited use, and then updates on a cyclical basis. Encyclopedias purchased through electronic licenses permit use of materials on a time-limited contract basis. Often encyclopedias in electronic format provide updates at a reduced rate. Online encyclopedias obviously have the potential of being updated more frequently. One must consider significant variations in cost when selecting print, CD-ROM, e-book, or online formats of encyclopedias (from free to thousands of dollars). Above all else, always consider the needs and abilities of the students served when selecting the most appropriate encyclopedias.

Basic Sources

GENERAL ENCYCLOPEDIAS

Since 1917, *World Book Encyclopedia* (World Book) has provided accuracy, objectivity, and reliability in research materials for both children and adults. This encyclopedia, which is available in print, CD-ROM, and online formats, provides a 22-volume set—online including state-of-the-art multimedia, editor-reviewed Web sites, and more. The CD-ROM version, *World Book Multimedia Encyclopedia*, contains the entire set of the printed encyclopedia, with the added advantage that all of its articles can be searched by keyword. The articles also contain hypertext links to other encyclopedia entries. Text can be downloaded or printed. The *World Book Multimedia Encyclopedia* also includes thousands of illustrations, several hundred maps, a few audio and video clips, and a dictionary. *World Book Online* is a premier online reference source containing every article from the print set plus thousands more, with state-of-the-art multimedia and editor-reviewed Web sites. It also includes *World Book Research Libraries*—primary and core source collections (books, documents, and selections) in major subject areas; and *Enciclopedia Estudiantil Hallazgos*, a basic Spanish-language encyclopedia for elementary and middle grades. World Book is noted for high standards of editorial excellence and technological developments that define the computer age.

Grolier Online Encyclopedia (go.grolier.com/) from Scholastic is an educational portal providing access to information from numerous electronic sources. This online suite consists of seven encyclopedias, with the foundation being three of the best-known encyclopedias: 1) The *New Book of Knowledge* (reference and current events for elementary readers and beyond); 2) *Grolier Multimedia Encyclopedia* (quick reference and news for middle and high school levels); and 3) *Encyclopedia Americana* (in-depth research and worldwide current events for middle school, high school, and college-age students). *La Nueva Enciclopedia Cumbre* is a comprehensive encyclopedia for Spanish speakers and language students. *Encyclopedia Britannica Online* (http://www.britannica .com/) offers a current and inclusive encyclopedia, which not only includes encyclopedia listings, but links to Web sites and articles as well. Another popular electronic encyclopedia, *Funk & Wagnall's New World Encyclopedia* (EBSCO) is available through the online database provider EBSCO*host*. This encyclopedia includes

Great Encyclopedias for Children (examples)

- *Childcraft: The How and Why Library*; (2000) World Book, Inc. (print with update annually, Childcraft Annual)
- *The Concise Animal Encyclopedia*; (2003) Kingfisher (print)
- *Concise Encyclopedia of the American Indian*; (2000) Random House (print)
- *First Science Encyclopedia*; (2008) DK Publishing (print)
- *e.encyclopedias*; (2008) DK Publishing (e-book)
- *Encyclopedia of Art for Young People*; (2008) Chelsea House/Infobase (print)
- *Encyclopedia of Native American Tribes*; (2006) Facts on File (print)
- *Encyclopedia of Vampires, Werewolves, and Other Monsters*; (2005) Facts on File (print)
- *Firefly Encyclopedia of Birds*; (2003) Firefly (print)
- *Illustrated Encyclopedia of Rocks of the World*; (2007) Lorenz/Anness (print)
- *Kid's Stuff*; (www.refdesk.com/kids.html)
- *The Kingfisher Science Encyclopedia*; (2006) Houghton Mifflin (print)
- *My First Britannica*; (2007) Encyclopedia Britannica (print)
- *My Very First Encyclopedia with Winnie the Pooh and Friends: Animals*; (2008) Disney Press (print)
- *The New Children's Encyclopedia*; (2009) DK Publishing (print)
- *New Encyclopedia of Snakes*; (2007) Princeton University Press (print)
- *Oxford Children's Encyclopedia*; (2004) Oxford University Press (print)
- *Oxford First Encyclopedia*; (2009) Oxford University Press (print)
- *Scholastic Children's Encyclopedia*; (2004) Scholastic (print)
- *Scholastic Encyclopedia of Animals*; (2004) Scholastic (print)
- *Scholastic Visual Sports Encyclopedia*; (2003) Scholastic (print)
- *The Usborne Internet-Linked Children's Encyclopedia*; (2004) Usborne (print)

a dictionary, thesaurus, atlases, news, and much more. *The Free Internet Encyclopedia* (http://www.cam-info.net/enc.html) is a mixture of other online resources. This Web site is divided into macro- and micro-pedias, both of which may be searched alphabetically. *Encyclopedia.com* (encyclopedia.com) is offered at no cost. This resource includes such subdivisions as dictionaries, thesaurus, almanacs, today in history, and much more.

Numerous additional print and electronic encyclopedias are available for your school library. The above are merely examples of the rich new world of encyclopedias for children through adults.

SINGLE VOLUME ENCYCLOPEDIAS

Single volume encyclopedias have seen a resurgence in popularity. These encyclopedias meet the needs of students interested in a single fact, place, or phenomenon. They are concise works of information that are excellent for ready-reference factual questions. The following are examples of single volume encyclopedias suitable for school library media centers: *Benet's Readers Encyclopedia*, fourth edition (long recognized as an outstanding reference concerning world literature); *Cambridge Encyclopedia* (one of the world's leading single-volume encyclopedias with an unrivaled reputation for its authority and reliability); *An Incomplete Education* (includes an astonishing amount of information that has become a classic among single-volume encyclopedias); *Cambridge Encyclopedia of the English Language* (understanding that English is the nearest thing we have to a world language, it includes a wealth of varieties, dialects, and traditions, all developing different ways and at different speeds); *Africana: The Encyclopedia of the African and African Experience* (prepared under the supervision of scholars Henry Louis Gates Jr. and Kwame Anthony Appiah, including more than 3,000 entries and scholarly articles about the history and culture of Africa and African Diaspora); *National Geographic Eyewitness to the 20th Century* (provides an extraordinary look at the most momentous and eventful issues in the history of humankind, including astonishing achievements, unparalleled horrors, and much more); as well as the *New Children's Encyclopedia*, *Scholastic Children's Encyclopedia*, and numerous other single-volume encyclopedias suitable for school libraries.

SUBJECT ENCYCLOPEDIAS

For every general encyclopedia available, dozens of subject works exist. Reviews of subject encyclopedias can be read in *Library Journal*, *Choice* (American Library Association), and *Booklist* (American Library Association) journals. An enormous number of subject encyclopedias are in existence, more than 1,000 in the English language alone. Subject encyclopedias contain detailed articles on particular topics, events, or even fields of study. These encyclopedias are particularly useful in research for providing explanations of individuals, concepts, techniques, vocabulary, events, and locations, as well as bibliographies regarding specialized topics that are not likely to be found in general encyclopedias. Subject encyclopedias may be single- or multi-volume works. Specialized encyclopedias from Facts on File for older students and *Eyewitness Books* by Dorling Kindersley for younger students are particularly appealing. The following are examples of subject encyclopedias that may spark student interest in a variety of topics: *Encyclopedia of Careers and Vocational Guidance* (Facts on File); *Encyclopedia of Espionage, Intelligence, and Security* (Thomson/ Gale); *Encyclopedia of Extreme Sports* (Greenwood); *Encyclopedia of the Holocaust*

(Macmillan); *Encyclopedia of World Religions* (Facts on File); *Encyclopedia of Food and Culture* (Scribner's); *Encyclopedia of African History and Culture* (Facts on File); *Encyclopedia of World War II* (Facts on File); *Encyclopedia of the Orient* (LexicOrient); *Encyclopedia Mythica* (Lindemans).

Merely search the Web and you will find an extraordinary amount of subject encyclopedias! Although it is important to evaluate online sources carefully, the following are some examples of online subject encyclopedias covering a variety of topics or areas of interest: E-Conflict World Encyclopedia and Simulation (http://www.emulateme.com/index.htm) profiles every nation and province of the world with maps and flags, quizzes, and numerous other links; Botany.com (http://www.botany.com/) is an encyclopedia of indoor and outdoor plants; Star Trek Voyager Encyclopedia (http://www.reocities.com/hollywood/9299/) allows one to pretend that they are voyagers, provides episode information, and includes an encyclopedia, A to Z, episode by episode); Encyclopedia Smithsonian (http://www.si.edu/Encyclopedia_SI/) offers answers to frequently asked questions about the Smithsonian, with links to resources on subjects from Art to Zoology; and many, many more to fill the research needs of your students.

Encyclopedias of all types are essential reference sources for school library media centers. General traditional, single volume, and subject encyclopedias provide answers, a systematic overview of selected topics—a picture of how things were and are.

Useful Web Sites

Country Reports
> www.emulateme.com
> *This site includes countries profiled from around the world—more than 6,000 pages and 6,000 related links on more than 200 countries with cultural, historical, and statistical country information.*

Encyclopedia.com
> http://www.encyclopedia.com/
> *This online source provides more than 60,000 frequently updated articles from the Columbia Encyclopedia; each article is enhanced with links to newspaper and magazine articles, pictures, and maps. Includes over 100 encyclopedias and dictionaries.*

Encyclopedia Britannica Online
> www.britannica.com
> *This online encyclopedia is fee based (but also included in many online databases); it is an encyclopedia that includes Britannica's Student and Concise Encyclopedias, the Web's best sites, multimedia, magazines, and much more.*

Encyclopedia Smithsonian
> http://www.si.edu/Encyclopedia
> *This site answers frequently asked questions about the Smithsonian, with links to resources on subjects from Art to Zoology.*

InfoPlease

    http://www.infoplease.com/encyclopedia/

    This site provides access to more than 57,000 articles from the Columbia Encyclopedia, sixth edition.

Surfnetkids Online Encyclopedias

    http://www.surfnetkids.com/encyclopedia.htm

    A list of online encyclopedias with reviews.

Wikipedia

    http://www.wikipedia.org/

    This is a popular collaboratively edited encyclopedia.

World Book Encyclopedia Online

    www.worldbookonline.com

    This online resource is fee based; it offers every article from the print set plus thousands more, including state-of-the art multimedia, editor-reviewed Web sites, and more.

Chapter 7

Geographical Sources

Introduction

Geographical reference sources can be thought of as works of art. They provide aesthetic satisfaction and the opportunity to let one's imagination wander. These reference materials are used primarily to answer location questions. Geographical sources may be used at an uncomplicated level (for example, Where is the country of Oman located?) or at a more sophisticated level involving relationships regarding environment, history, climate, and political boundaries (for example, How has the melting of the polar ice caps affected the climate in the Northern Hemisphere?). Human society has become more global than ever before; therefore, recent geographical resources are a necessity. When a student requests the identification of a geographic place, normally the answer can be found online, in an atlas, or an individual map.

Some questions may require extremely up-to-date geographical materials— atlases, maps, and other resources should be specifically selected for current event–type questions. Responding to the need for current information may require the use of online resources. Another category of geographical questions includes historical ones. Information of this nature can be located in older atlases and related geographical sources. Therefore, age need not be a primary criterion when weeding geographical materials. Geographical requests can vary widely, requiring an assortment of geography-related sources such as current, historical, and thematic atlases, maps of varying types, gazetteers, travel guides, and even general reference materials that include geographic information such as encyclopedias. With the wealth of geographical sources currently online, it is now significantly less complicated to fulfill the diverse requests required by students. The categories of geographical sources considered in this chapter include print and electronic: maps, atlases, gazetteers, and other general geographical sources appropriate for school library media centers.

Maps are representations of certain boundaries on a flat surface. However, there are a wide variety of maps designed for every purpose, from indicating soil content to determining the vegetation in a particular city via satellite imaging. A physical map traces the different features of the land from rivers and valleys to mountains and hills.

A street (route) map shows roads, railroads, bridges, and similar phenomena. A map depicting specific conditions is typically referred to as a thematic map. These, either separately or as one, make up a large number of maps found in atlases. An atlas is simply a volume of maps. Atlases can provide, at a nominal cost, maps of the whole world in one book. Individual atlases include numerous subjects and offer reference information on geographical features, oceans, space, and historical and political geography of particular areas. Atlases may be divided into three categories: current, historical, and thematic. Gazetteers or geographic dictionaries provide information regarding geographic place-names. Often they include information on such topics as population, climate, and economy. Electronic geographic sources are becoming a vitally important part of school library media reference resources. These sources serve a multitude of valuable functions, are typically user friendly, and are remarkably current. Often electronic and print geographic materials complement each other; this chapter will discuss all formats of geographic resources.

Evaluation and Selection

Evaluation of Geographic Sources

PUBLISHER (AUTHORITY)
- It is best to purchase from a reputable publisher of geographic materials.
- If the publisher's reputation is unknown, review other works it has published.

SCALE
- Understand that scale is the most important element, as it defines the amount of information that can be shown.
- The scale should be clearly defined and appropriate for the intended audience.

CURRENCY
- Our geographic world is changing rapidly!
- A five-year-old atlas is considered historical.
- Internet sources should provide the date of the last update.
- Hyperlinks that are broken would be an indicator that the electronic format is not updated.

INDEXING
- An effective geographical index is an alphabetical list of all place-names that appear on the map.
- A comprehensive index is important.
- Electronic geographical sources should provide rapid and user-friendly access to information.

FORMAT
- Regardless of the format, the resources must provide the desired information quickly and easily and be clear and legible.

Geographic sources may be evaluated using many of the same criteria as other reference sources; however, there are several additional points to consider. Because these materials depend on graphic arts and mathematics as well, further issues should be noted regarding evaluation and selection. The basic criteria to be considered when evaluating geographic resources include publisher (authority), scale, currency, indexing, and format.

As with any reference area, there exist competent and reputable publishers in the field. This is also true of geographic sources. In the United States, the leading publishers include Rand McNally and the National Geographic Society. A prominent international publisher is Oxford University Press. When the publisher's reputation is unknown, it is best to determine other works it may have published. This is particularly important when considering electronic geographic sources, where the vendor or publisher may differ from standard companies. Numerous smaller firms also produce geographic materials, in particular, city maps. In all cases it is best to purchase resources from reliable publishers or locally reputable organizations. It should also be noted that geography is a component of numerous other reference materials such as encyclopedias and almanacs. It is important that the publisher of the encyclopedia or other materials has a reliable reputation as well.

Scale is a characteristic that makes geographic resources different from other reference materials. Maps are usually classed according to scales. They must be drawn to scale such that accurate comparisons may be distinguished between a verbal scale and a representative fraction. One unit on a map equals a particular number of units on the ground (for example, one inch equals 10 miles). Scale is the most important element of a map, as it defines the amount of information that can be shown, as well as the size of the geographic area. The scale from map to map in a given atlas may vary widely, although better atlases attempt to standardize their work. An effective map or atlas identifies the scale; as a school librarian it is important that you decide the appropriate scale for your student population.

Another essential criterion for geographic resources is currency. Because the world is changing so rapidly, it is of utmost importance that the school library provides up-to-date geographical information. School librarians should update their world maps frequently, although electronic formats are now supplying current information on a regular basis. A world atlas that is five years old portrays enough obsolete information to be considered only for historical purposes. A multitude of changes occurs on a continual basis regarding geographical sources—place-names, boundaries, roads, and so forth. Revisions of maps and atlases (completely overhauled and developed) normally take place every 10 years—the span of time between the American census.

An effective geographical index is an alphabetical list of all place-names that appear on the map. A comprehensive index is as important in geographic reference works as the maps themselves. In addition, there should be a reference to the exact map as well as latitude, longitude, and grid information. Indexes may also include such items as national parks, mountains, and historical sites. An effective atlas or map indexes as many features as possible. Online and electronic software should provide rapid and user-friendly access to the information it includes.

Geographic sources in any format should provide the desired information as quickly and easily as possible; it must be clear and legible. Maps with fewer items of information are typically easier to read; the actual number of points represented on a map is a major editorial decision. Electronic geographical sources are growing increasingly important and necessary. There are numerous high-quality and user-friendly electronic materials. National Geographic's online site (www.national geographic.com/maps/index.html) is an excellent source offering many useful features. Rand McNally's online site (www.randmcnally.com) is also a valuable source for planning trips, exploring maps, and finding addresses and driving directions. The format of geographical sources should be selected on the basis of student needs and abilities, as well as relative cost.

As with the selection of all reference materials, each school library media specialist must determine the informational requirements and desires of the school, student population, and community served. This is also true of the appropriate selection and evaluation of geographical materials. However, locating suitable selection tools and aids in this field is more difficult than other reference areas. Several journals provide reviews of geographical sources (some on a regular basis, some sporadically) such as *Booklist* (American Library Association), *Library Media Connection* (Linworth Publishing), *Library Journal* (MediaSource), and *School Library Journal* (MediaSource).

Basic Sources

CURRENT WORLD ATLASES

Current atlases are required for up-to-date information on geographical and political changes in the world. Many students find print versions of atlases enjoyable as well as useful. Probably the most notable single-volume world atlas (print format) is the *Times Atlas of the World* (HarperCollins). The *Times Atlas of the World* is divided into three basic sections: an introduction with general physical information; the atlas proper with a series of regional maps; and a final index-gazetteer section. The *National Geographic World Atlas for Young Explorers* (National Geographic Magazine) is available in print with a companion interactive Web site. This atlas is best suited for middle school students. The *World Almanac Children's Atlas* is designed for younger students with more than 30 separate nations and regions maps, full color photographs, and an index.

An atlas suitable for school libraries is the *National Geographic Atlas* (National Geographic Society). This atlas contains excellent thematic maps, graphics, and vivid comparisons between places of the world. *Goode's World Atlas* (Rand McNally), a desk-size atlas in print format, is reasonably priced and easy to use. This atlas is often found in school libraries. Goode's is revised every other year and contains a serviceable index with nearly 40,000 entries.

An excellent online atlas is the National Atlas of the United States (www .nationalatlas.gov) created by the U.S. government, which allows you to customize maps using their map maker. It allows for investigation of layers using map layers. It allows for printing of maps in their selection of printable maps. There is also a link to dynamic maps as well as a link to order wall maps. Some online atlases are an integrated part of other reference sources such as *Grolier's Encyclopedia* (Scholastic; go-elem.grolier.com/sframe). Other examples of online atlases are the Map Machine Atlas (http://education.nationalgeographic.com/education/mapping/), World Atlas (www.worldatlas.com), and World Atlas and Map Library (www.infoplease.com/atlas/). A popular source for maps and directions is Google Maps (maps.google.com). Google also provides the Google Earth (earth.google.com) desktop and mobile applications to explore the earth and the sky in 3D.

HISTORICAL ATLASES

Historical atlases are necessary for the study of early exploration, boundary changes, and military campaigns. The Historical Atlas of the 20th Century, an online source (www.erols.com/mwhite28/20centry.htm) charts socioeconomic trends, systems of government, cities, and wars throughout the 20th century.

Numerous additional historical atlases are appropriate and useful for school libraries. They vary in content, concentrating on either particular periods in history or specific regions. Examples of historical atlases suitable for school libraries include *Atlas of American History* and *Historical Atlas of the World*, both published by Rand McNally. *Atlas of World History* (www.atlasofworldhistory.com) covers Africa, Asia, and Europe to the year 1000. Facts on File (www.factsonfile.com) produces several historical atlases including *Atlas of African-American History* and *Atlas of American History* both suited for high school students. Both are available in print and e-book formats. *Atlas of African American History* includes 70 full-color maps and important cultural, historical, political, and social events in African American history in four volumes. *Atlas of American History* is divided into 10 chronological sections that cover military history, migration, and religious history. It makes an excellent resource for studying American history.

THEMATIC ATLASES

Thematic atlases emphasize a specific subject or region. They currently represent a new trend in atlas publishing. Although they are considered atlases, many thematic atlases more closely resemble finely illustrated popular histories.

The National Geographic Society produces several thematic atlases, which include *Atlas of the Civil War*. This atlas contains 85 rare maps of the time, 320 documentary photos, and various battlefield sketches. The *African Adventure Atlas* is organized by geographical regions. It includes facts about each country as well as cultural attractions and historical sites. The *National Geographic Atlas of the Middle East* contains maps and profiles for Afghanistan, Pakistan, and Sudan. It also includes historical and cultural information.

MAPS

At least 90 percent of the maps published each year originate from government sources. The United States Geological Survey (USGS) is the agency officially responsible for domestic mapping. Of all the USGS series, the topographical maps are the best known and most often used. The maps show in great detail the physical features of an area. Topographical maps can be downloaded free from their Web site. USGS also allows you to customize a map of America by using the link to the National Atlas of the United States. To get an update of their quadrangle topographical map you can use US Topo, their digital format for maps. There is also a link to download historical topographical maps.

Most municipal governments and regional agencies produce maps for planning and engineering studies; they are typically free or are available at a reasonable reproduction cost. Chambers of commerce usually have detailed city maps, as well as other information on the city itself; they are excellent resources for library media centers. State departments of tourism are also good sources of maps, which can be found online (for instance, the online source for Kentucky is www.kentuckytourism .com). Many online sites exist for maps of all kinds. It is important to remember, however, that it is sometimes difficult to "get the big picture" on a computer screen. In addition, printing can be a challenge. Nonetheless, these resources are typically free of charge and valuable resources for school libraries.

When evaluating a local map, the following should be considered: Is it truly local? Does it show the area in detail? Is it large scale? Is it current? Is it appropriate for student use?

GAZETTEERS AND OTHER GEOGRAPHICAL SOURCES

A gazetteer is a list of geographical names and/or physical features. It is a geographical dictionary for finding lists of cities, mountains, rivers, populations, and other features. Almost every atlas includes a gazetteer as an appendix that is used to locate the place-names in that volume. Atlas gazetteers are primarily useful for locating major towns, cities, administrative divisions, and physical features. Gazetteers differ from the index to an atlas in that they are generally more comprehensive. The U.S. Gazetteer, available online (www.census.gov/geo/www/gazetteer/gazette.html), is an excellent example of an electronic gazetteer, identifying locations via name, state, or zip code. The World Gazetteer (world-gazetteer.com) provides population data and other statistics arranged by country. The Columbia Gazetteer of the World (www .columbiagazetteer.org/) is a subscription-based gazetteer aimed at high schools and higher education.

Geography has supplementary reference sources that contain information not found in atlases, maps, and gazetteers. Rand McNally (www.randmcnally.com), MapQuest (www.mapquest.com/), Google Maps (http://maps.google.com), and Bing Maps (www.bing.com/maps/) are examples of online street maps that enable one to find a specific location and obtain driving directions or plan a trip to that destination.

Travel guidebooks are also purposeful geographical resources for school libraries. These sources deal with down-to-earth facts about specific locations. The most notable publishers of travel guidebooks include Frommer, Fodor, Fielding, and Dorling Kindersley.

As stimulating as geographic materials are for the imaginative mind, they are also an invaluable part of any school library reference collection. As a school librarian, you will find that there are as many reasons for consulting geographic resources as there are students in your school. With the introduction of electronic maps and atlases, reference work involving geographic materials is both an exciting and challenging part of reference sources and services for school librarians.

Additional Online Geographical Resources

General Geographical Sources

Country at a Glance
> http://cyberschoolbus.un.org/infonation/index.asp
> *United Nations data including flag, latitude and longitude, area, population, population density, capital city, languages, largest city, currency, UN membership date, GDP, and GDP per capita. The companion site, Infonation, allows one to view and compare statistical data for the Member States of the United Nations.*
> *scope: international*
> *publisher: United Nations Publications*

World Climate: Weather, Rainfall, and Temperature Data
> http://www.worldclimate.com
> *Historical weather data, providing monthly mean average over a range of years.*
> *scope: more than 85,000 records*
> *publisher: Robert Hoare, Buttle and Tuttle*

The World Factbook
> https://www.cia.gov/library/publications/the-world-factbook/
> *Online edition of the World Factbook, compiled by the CIA for the U.S. Government. Country profiles cover geography, people, government, economy, communications, transportation, military, and transnational issues.*
> *scope: international, the Factbook is updated weekly*
> *publisher: Central Intelligence Agency*

World Flag Database
> http://www.flags.net/
> *Descriptions and illustrations of flags for countries, territories, subnational regions, and international organizations. Includes national and state flags, ensigns, and subnational flags. The Flag Institute created the original graphics.*
> *scope: more than 260 entries covering hundreds of flags*
> *publisher: World Flag Database and Graham Bartram*

GAZETTEERS

GEOnet Names Server
> http://earth-info.nga.mil/gns/html/index.html

(continues)

*The U.S. National Imagery and Mapping Agency's (NIMA) database
of foreign geographic feature names as approved by the U.S. Board on
Geographic Names. Provides latitude, longitude, area, and UTM and JOG
number. Note, you must know the country in which the feature is located.
scope: 3.5 million entries; worldwide excluding the United States and
Antarctica
publisher: National Imagery and Mapping Agency*

Getty Thesaurus of Geographic Names
http://www.getty.edu/research/conducting_research/vocabularies/tgn/
*A structured vocabulary with an emphasis on art and architecture,
covering continents, nations, historical places, and physical features.
Each record includes geographic coordinates, notes, sources for the data,
and the role of the place (e.g., inhabited place, state capital). Names can
include vernacular, English, other languages, historical names, natural
order, and inverted order.
scope: around one million entries; current and historical; international
publisher: Getty Research Institute*

Place Names on the Internet
http://libguides.asu.edu/content.php?pid=10928&sid=79050
*Portal to place name servers; arranged in World, Country, and Planetary
sections.
scope: Portal
publisher: Arizona State University Libraries*

ATLASES AND MAPS

Peakware World Relief Maps
http://www.peakware.com/
*3D interactive relief maps of continents, mountain ranges, and specific
peaks. Part of the Peakware World Mountain Encyclopedia, which includes
photographs, live Web cams, and summit logs.
scope: world
publisher: Peakware*

World Time Zone Map
http://aa.usno.navy.mil/faq/docs/world_tzones.html
*H.M. Nautical Almanac Office map of standard time zones, corrected to
January 2012, with legend for universal time.
scope: world
publisher: U.S. Naval Observatory*

Webliography

Google Maps
> http://maps.google.com/
> _This is an online street map that enables one to find a specific location and obtain driving directions or plan a trip to a specific destination._

Grolier's Encyclopedia
> http://go-elem.grolier.com/sframe
> _Grolier's Encyclopedia includes an extremely useful atlas for schools._

The Historical Atlas of the 20th Century
> http://users.erols.com/mwhite28/20centry.htm
> _This online atlas charts socioeconomic trends, systems of government, cities, and wars throughout the 20th century._

Kentucky Tourism Map
> http://www.kentuckytourism.com/
> _This Web site provides geographical information for the state of Kentucky._

The Lonely Planet
> http://www.lonelyplanet.com
> _Lonely Planet provides maps and travel information._

Map Maker Interactive
> http://education.nationalgeographic.com/education/mapping/interactive-map/?ar_a=1
> _Map Maker Interactive is a universally known and recommended online atlas._

MapQuest
> http://www.mapquest.com
> _This is an online street map that enables one to find a specific location and obtain driving directions or plan a trip to a specific destination._

National Geographic
> http://www.nationalgeographic.com/maps/
> _This useful online site offers Atlas Maps, Flags and Facts, and much more._

Rand McNally
> www.randmcnally.com
> _This Web site is a valuable source for planning trips, exploring maps, and finding addresses and driving lessons._

The U.S. Gazetteer
> http://www.census.gov/geo/www/gazetteer/gazette.html
> _This online source is an excellent example of an electronic gazetteer, identifying locations via name, state, or zip code._

Chapter *8*

Electronic Indexes and Abstracts; Periodical and Specialized Databases

Introduction

Indexes, whether separate guides to periodical articles or part of books, are used to reveal specific portions of information in a larger unit. An index is an analysis of a document, typically by subject. An effective index includes enough access points to allow the user to locate precisely what is needed.

Abstracts are an extension of indexes. They present a brief, objective summary of the content, and serve as an aid in assessing the content of a document. Abstracts provide enough information to give the user an accurate idea about the subject area. They are usually descriptive, as opposed to evaluative. A typical abstract is from 100 to 300 words in length. An effective abstract, by itself, may include more than enough information to answer a ready-reference question.

Because information in indexes and abstracts is often time sensitive, they are commonly found online as an integrated part of the growing number of online full-text information databases. Some of the largest information databases incorporating indexes and abstracts are online periodical databases containing articles from academic journals, newspapers, popular magazines, and other sources, all of which are searchable by subject headings and keywords. Typically a periodical database will contain a searchable index of articles, each of which is described in an abstract. Some abstracts will also have a link to the full-text version of the article. Large periodical databases such as EBSCO contain a number of different collections of electronic indexes organized by broad topics such as current events, science, or the humanities. Again, while most of the indexes contain abstracts, they may or may not have links to full text articles. Electronic formats have numerous advantages, such as rapid search of a number of indexes, the ability to move from citation to abstract to full text, and the availability of more points of access through keywords in the title, text, or a specific periodical.

Evaluation and Selection

Evaluation of Indexes and Abstracts

ACCURACY
- Check that all major facets of the content in the article are represented by entries in the subject index.
- All authors affiliated with the indexed item should be included in the author index.
- Author names should be spelled identically in both the index and the work itself.
- Subjects should represent the content of the publication.
- Effective abstracts should depict an accurate summary of the original article's content.

AUTHORITY
- Remember that authority primarily relies on the reputation of the publisher or sponsoring agency; two prominent publishers include EBSCO and ProQuest.
- For electronic resources, the authority should be verified by talking to subject experts and reading appropriate reviews.
- The publisher or vender should supply the necessary documentation, frequent updates, and information regarding current changes.

FORMAT
- When evaluating electronic sources, it is essential to consider both ease of searching and standardized procedures throughout all of the vendor's or publisher's indexes.
- Readability of entries is essential for both print and electronic formats. Consider the size of type, use of abbreviations and symbols, and font style.

(continues)

Indexes and abstracts should be evaluated and selected such that they best reveal the contents of the collection, or will refer students to appropriate information not found in the school library. Evaluation of print or electronic indexes and abstracts follows much of the same rules as other reference sources. The basic difference lies in the ease of retrieval of data. The following criteria should be used when evaluating indexes and abstracts: accuracy, authority, format, and scope.

A misleading index or inaccurate abstract can cause a multitude of problems. Accuracy is an essential factor in evaluating these resources. It should be ascertained that all major facets of the content in the article are represented by entries in the subject index, and that all authors affiliated with the indexed item are included in the author index. Additionally, author names should be spelled the same way in both the index and the work itself. Subjects should represent the content of the publication, and cross-references should be included as needed. Effective abstracts depict an accurate summary of the original article's content, written by the author of the article or by a third party (for example, the abstract's publishing staff).

The authority of indexes and abstracts relies on the reputation of the publisher or sponsoring agency. Four prominent publishers of indexes are EBSCO, H. W. Wilson, ProQuest, and University Microfilms International (UMI). As more electronic indexes appear, additional publishers will emerge; talking to subject experts and reading appropriate reviews should verify their reputation. It is also important with electronic resources to consider the reputation of the vendor and the producer of the product (which may not be the same as the publisher). The publisher or vendor should supply the necessary documentation, frequent updates, and information regarding current changes.

In evaluating indexes and abstracts it is essential to consider both ease of searching and standardized procedures throughout the entire vendor's or publisher's indexes. Because some databases do not cover material before the mid-1960s, printed versions may be required for searching older literature. Readability of entries is also essential for both print and electronic formats. The size of type, use of abbreviations and symbols, and the use of boldface type should be appropriate and effective. Arrangement is another consideration when evaluating indexes and abstracts, although with electronic sources, the search engine will normally reveal the location of a term regardless of its location.

The scope of indexes and abstracts should be discovered. Does the index or abstract adequately cover the materials in the field of interest? Frequency of publication and cumulation should also be taken into account. Typically, however, electronic indexes and abstracts are automatically cumulated. Other considerations are the number of subjects covered and the types of materials indexed. Indexes and abstracts differ in the number of publications included and the depth of the index provided. Some of these sources are quite inclusive regarding the types of materials indexed, while others restrict their coverage to particular titles. As there are many indexes available today, be aware of possible duplications and overlaps in information.

The selection of indexes and abstracts for a school library depends on the needs of the students and the characteristics of the current library collection. Many standard resources will serve as aids in the selection of indexes and abstracts. One example is the *Guide to Reference Materials for School Media Centers* (Libraries Unlimited). Additionally, review journals such as the following will include information on indexes and abstracts: *Booklist* (American Library Association), *Library Media Connection* (Linworth Publishing), *Choice* (American Library Association), *Library Journal* (Reed Publishing), and *School Library Journal* (Reed Publishing). Cost and student needs are the most critical factors when selecting indexes and abstracts. The price of these resources is an important issue due to the fact that they are usually quite expensive. Additionally, a school library will typically require relatively few indexes. It is also important to consider whether the index will provide full-text articles. An index is of little use when the library does not have access to the periodicals indexed. Abstracts are typically only helpful for brief facts, ready-reference–type questions. The cost of electronic databases can be difficult to understand. Different publishers and vendors vary in their pricing options. Licensing is a factor in determining cost as well. Vendors and publishers differ in their approaches as to how much a school library is charged, depending on the number of users and how they are using the system. The indexes and abstracts purchased should reflect the types of information the students need access to and the student demand for information. General periodical and newspaper indexes are normally required in school libraries. Currently, with the availability of online indexes and abstracts, access to numerous additional indexes is possible without specific subscriptions. In addition, many school libraries now have online indexes and abstracts available through library consortia, such as statewide library networks.

Basic Sources

The focus of these resources is current, well-known indexes and abstracts appropriate for school library situations. These sources provide the access to higher-quality information (than a typical Web search, for instance). They are divided into two categories: online periodical indexes and specialized indexes and databases. As there are countless indexes and abstracts available today, the following are merely examples. The following series—ProQuest, SIRS, EBSCO, H. W. Wilson, NewsBank, and LexisNexis databases—are fee-based services.

ONLINE PERIODICAL INDEXES

One popular publisher of indexes is ProQuest/Cambridge Information Group; their most well-known indexes are the ProQuest series. These indexes are offered online (http://Proquestk12.com). The ProQuest collection allows users to quickly and easily locate magazines, newspapers, and topical reference information. It is delivered in abstract and full text. The following are examples of the resources included in the ProQuestK12 collection: eLibrary, with over 2,500 full-text magazines, newspapers, reference books, and multimedia searchable by subject, date, or Lexile level; ProQuestCentralK12, containing over 8,000 full-text scholarly journals, magazines, and newspapers; and the Social Issues Resource (SIRS), providing integrated access to thousands of full-text articles from magazines, scholarly journals, newspapers, and government documents related to topical issues.

EBSCO is another leading publisher of indexes and abstracts available online for the high school, middle school, and elementary grade levels (www.ebscohost.com/schools). The Primary Online package includes four collections with over 80 full-text magazines, photos, maps, and flags, the *Encyclopedia of Animals*, *Funk & Wagnall's New World Encyclopedia*, and the *American Heritage Children's Dictionary*, all searchable using the child-friendly Searchasaurus interface. The Middle Online Package uses this search interface for access to more than 150 full-text periodicals, 131,000 full-text biographies, and over 100,000 primary source documents by keyword or general subjects such as Literature, Sports, and Nature. This package also includes Topic Search, a current events database of over 150,000 articles, biographies, public opinion polls, book reviews, pamphlets, and government information. The High School collection is comprised of six databases (Consumer Health Complete, Education Research Complete, ERIC, MAS Complete, Newspaper Source Plus, TOPICsearch) of full-text articles on topics ranging from Advance Placement to World History. MAS Complete provides full-text for more than 500 magazines, over 400 reference titles, and thousands of biographies, photos, maps, and primary source documents, and includes Points of View Reference Center, a database of articles covering both sides of a current issue.

H. W. Wilson (http://www.ebscohost.com/wilson) now a part of EBSCO, is a leading publisher of indexes and abstracts in specialized areas such as business, education, and science, many of which have the option of access to full-text articles. Wilson databases also include collection development tools such as Children's, Middle and Junior High, High, Fiction, Graphic Novels, and Non-book Core Collections. The merger of the two providers has resulted in the development of seven "super databases" offering access to thousands of full-text articles in art, education, the humanities, applied science and technology, law, library and information science, and biography.

NewsBank is yet another popular indexing series (www.newsbank.com/schools/). NewsBank's KidsPage and Connections for Kids contain an easy-to-search database of articles, activities, and lesson plans for the elementary and middle grades, covering key issues and events in every subject area. Additional resources for middle and high school students include index, abstract, and full-text information in the following databases: Access World News—world's largest full-text news database; ScienceSource Collection—comprehensive coverage of science concepts; Acceda Noticias—Spanish-language national and international newspapers; Archive of Americana—primary source documents for American history; Statbank—numerical data for a variety of subject; UN Connections—international issues and events; and newspaper archives from across the United States. Many of the newsbank resources also offer curriculum support, alignment with curriculum standards, and Lexile levels.

SPECIALIZED INDEXES AND DATABASES

As with general indexes and abstracts, there exist a multitude of specialized indexes and databases covering a wide range of subjects. The following are examples of specialized indexes and databases appropriate for school libraries.

The Educational Resources Information Center (ERIC) is a federally funded national information system that provides a variety of services and products on a broad range of education-related issues (http://www.eric.ed.gov/). It is the world's largest source of educational information and contains more than one million abstracts of documents and journal articles on educational research and practice. This online database is updated monthly; the information is timely and accurate. ERIC may be consulted for both original and secondary material on education. The system includes: 1) an index to unpublished reports and an index to journals that indexes approximately 800 periodicals in education; 2) an ongoing subject vocabulary represented in the frequently updated Thesaurus; and 3) a decentralized organizational structure for acquiring and processing the documents that are indexed and abstracted and full-text access to over 300,000 items.

Each entry in ERIC has a narrative abstract of approximately 200 words; authors write the abstracts. Documents include proceedings from research conferences, speeches, technical reports, dissertations, curriculum guides, educational legislation, and lesson plans prepared for the classroom.

Numerous online sources provide guides to newspapers and magazines. Examples of these include the Internet Public Library Newspapers & Magazines section, which contains links to national, state, and international periodicals (http://www.ipl.org/div/news/). Newspapers Online (www.newspapers.com/) is yet another valuable source that includes free access to the top 100 worldwide and local newspapers.

The Children's Magazine Guide published by Libraries Unlimited (http://www.childrensmag.com/) is a useful online index for children ages 8 to 12. This resource includes approximately 60 popular children's magazines, providing articles on sports, science, popular culture, and current events. A beginner's tutorial helps students get started with the index.

There are several government and nongovernmental organization (NGO) indexes and databases of value to school libraries. The Federal Resources for Educational Excellence (http://www.free.ed.gov/), the Government Printing Office (www.gpo.gov), and Science.gov (http://www.science.gov/) contain full-text public records from a variety of federal agencies that are searchable by title, date, subject, and keyword. Important information about other countries and international development targeted toward the K–12 community can be found through databases from NGOs such as the United Nations (http://www.un.org/Pubs/CyberSchoolBus/) and the World Bank (http://youthink.worldbank.org/).

There are also a number of specialized indexes that are available online through subscriptions. The Columbia Granger's Index to Poetry (Columbia University Press) provides an index to more than 250,000 poems and includes a subject index with approximately 6,000 categories. An interesting feature of Granger's is the inclusion of thousands of last lines, which is a valuable tool when searching for quotations (http://www.columbiagrangers.org/). The Play Index (EBSCO/H.W. Wilson) has published more than 31,000 individual plays from 1949 to the present. Of importance to school libraries, the Play Index uses tags, "c" for children through grade 6, and "y" for young adults in grades 7 through 12 (http://www.ebscohost.com/academic/play-index).

The average school library will typically not require more than one general index due to prohibitive cost, and repetition and overlap among indexes. Prior to purchase, review materials should be consulted and discussions with vendors should occur, as well as hands-on experiences with the indexes themselves.

Webliography

Children's Magazine Guide
>   http://cmg.lu.com/default.jsp
>   *This online database Children's Magazine Guide Online provides access to fiction and nonfiction articles from more than 65 children's magazines.*

Columbia Granger's World of Poetry
>   http://www.columbiagrangers.org/
>   *The Columbia Granger's World of Poetry contains 250,000 poems in full text and 450,000 citations and is continuously updated.*

EBSCO/H. W. Wilson
>   http://www.ebscohost.com/
>   *One of the largest providers of online information, EBSCO products include online periodical databases, reference titles, and e-books, designed specifically for the K–12 community. EBSCO offers the Play Index from H. W. Wilson.*

Educational Resources Information Center (ERIC)
>   http://eric.ed.gov
>   *The ERIC database uses the latest search and retrieval methods to cull education literature and provide high-quality access to educators, researchers, and the general public.*

Federal Resources for Educational Excellence
>   http://www.free.ed.gov/
>   *This Web source is extremely useful and inclusive, containing such areas as the Arts, Educational Technology, Foreign Languages, Physical Education, Language Arts, Science, Mathematics, Social Studies, Vocational Education, and so forth.*

Internet Public Library News & Magazines
>   http://www.ipl.org/div/news/
>   *The IPL includes magazines, e-zines, and others on topics such as Arts and Humanities, Education, Reference, and others.*

NewsBank Online Database
>   http://www.newsbank.com/schools
>   *NewsBank Online Database is a reputable, user-friendly online source for K–12 students.*

Newspapers Online
>   http://www.newspapers.com/
>   *This is an inclusive resource that contains national and international newspapers, and links to other media outlets.*

ProQuest Online Database
> http://www.proquest.com/
>
> *ProQuest online information service provides access to thousands of current periodicals and newspapers, many updated daily and containing full-text articles from 1986. Proquest offers the SIRS online database.*

Science.gov
> http://www.science.gov
>
> *Science.gov is a portal for government science information including over 50 scientific databases, 200 million pages of science information, and over 2,100 scientific Web sites.*

United Nations Cyberschoolbus
> http://cyberschoolbus.un.org/
>
> *K–12 portal to online information from the United Nations.*

United States Government Printing Office (GPO)
> www.gpo.gov/
>
> *The U.S. Government Printing Office disseminates official information from all three branches of the federal government.*

World Bank youthink!
> http://youthink.worldbank.org/4kids/
>
> *Information on global issues from World Bank experts on international development.*

PART 3

The Art of Questioning

Chapter *9*

The Reference Interview

Introduction

One of the primary functions of a school library media specialist is to assist students in the use of the library and its collections. As a school library media specialist, you must determine what the students want. This process is referred to as the *reference interview*; it is an essential part of reference services and a major function of all school librarians. The reference interview is fundamentally a conversation between the school library media specialist and the student, for the purpose of clarifying the student's needs and aiding in meeting those needs (determining what they want). It is distinguished from general conversation between the school library media specialist and the student because it has a specific purpose and structure. In the reference interview, the school library media specialist's goals are to determine efficiently and productively the nature, quantity, and level of information the student requires, as well as the most appropriate format. The effective reference interview takes practice and creativity; this process can efficiently connect knowledge with the student's information needs. It is critical that school librarians learn to listen and communicate more effectively with students.

In discussing the reference interview, it is virtually impossible to divorce human relations from communications skills. It is vital to remember that school librarians bring students and information together. It is up to each school library media specialist to ensure that everything possible is done to keep the channels of communication open and flowing. *Empowering Learners* views one role of the school library media specialist as a teacher collaborating with students to build information literacy skills and identify appropriate tools for collecting, communicating, finding, and using information (AASL, 2009, 20).

As important as school librarians are to students, students are equally as important to school librarians, for they are the lifeblood of our profession. Each school library media specialist brings a distinctive personality and unique characteristics to the reference interview process. How these personalities and characteristics, both the school library media specialist's and the student's, affect the interview procedure is crucial. As school librarians, interviewing techniques should be refined and interpersonal skills improved on a continual basis. The reference interview bridges the communication gap between the student and the school library media specialist.

In order to properly perform any reference service, the school library media specialist must have an exceptional knowledge of the library media center's collection. Familiarity with resources, both print and nonprint, provides students with accurate and appropriate information. In addition to knowledge of reference materials, the school library media specialist should possess a complete knowledge of the general collection, as well as community resources.

Because questions differ, types of interviews vary also, as well as responses provided (from short and to the point to long and detailed). A successful reference interview is tailored to meet each student's needs. As school librarians, the types of interviews that occur most frequently are Ready-Reference, Research Projects, and Readers' Advisory. Each type of interview possesses its own unique qualities; however, all types fundamentally link knowledge with student needs—learning.

Appropriate reference interviews consist of rules, methods, and characteristics that create the accurate connection between information and the needs of students. Reference interviewing is not only an art, but also a science. It can be learned and practiced to produce effective results for students.

The Patron—The Student

One of the most important aspects of the reference process (if not the most important) is attitude—how the student perceives his question will be received. It sets the mood for the entire transaction. It is important that the reference interview is comprehended as a two-way communications system.

It has been observed that the deepest principle of human nature (young or old) is the desire to be appreciated. By keeping this in mind, work as a reference interviewer will be remarkably easier. As varied as the students' reasons and levels are when asking questions, they have the same basic need—to protect or strengthen their self-concept. The school library media specialist should know as much about the student (social data) as possible in order to conduct the most appropriate and effective reference interview. This is not always easy, nor even possible. However, school librarians are in an exclusive position that allows them to gather data about their population prior to interviewing. Nevertheless, during the interview, it may also be necessary to employ substitutes in order to obtain information, verbal and nonverbal cues, as well as other predictive devices, which expectantly discover what the student wants.

Each student comes to the reference interview with a distinctive question, as well as an individual personality. There are, however, basic considerations regarding students that are helpful when conducting a reference interview:

- The student may not know what to expect, or the precise reaction the school library media specialist will have to the question.

- The average student may have no pre-knowledge of the type of resource(s) that will answer his or her question.
- The student's communications skills may not be as refined as the school library media specialist's.
- The student may not know the terminology (library lingo) used in the reference interview.
- The student may not specifically know what he or she is searching for, due to lack of knowledge concerning the subject or the particular assignment.
- The student may have a lack of knowledge regarding the library media center (collection) and usage (policies) of the library media center.
- The student may misinterpret the school library media specialist's nonverbal and verbal cues.
- The student may be fearful of the school library media specialist and/or certain technologies or frustrated about the question being raised.

As a school library media specialist, remain aware that the reference interview is a two-way communications system. Communications may become miscommunications when a student is unable to verbalize his or her information need. As described by Kuhlthau, "The bibliographic paradigm is based on certainty and order, whereas [students'] problems are characterized by uncertainty and confusion" (1991, 361). The school library media specialist is in the position of fostering communications; discovering, understanding, and mastering the effective art and science of reference interviewing; and connecting knowledge with students' information needs.

The Setting

The physical setting in which the reference interview occurs affects its potential success. The environment of the school library media center conveys a message to the students. School librarians have some degree of control over the design and appearance of the library media center, in particular, the reference collection (both print and nonprint) as well as the physical setting. Maximization of comfort and utility are of foremost significance. The following points should be considered with regard to the physical setting of the library as it applies to the reference interview:

- Reference interviews should take place in a relatively quiet, uninterrupted area of the library media center that is comfortable and free of clutter.
- The reference area, the space in which the reference interview is conducted, should contain proper seating and be located near both print and nonprint reference sources.
- Reference materials should be organized in such a manner that the school library media specialist and the student can easily and quickly locate reference sources during and after the reference interview.

The reference interview is a critical component of successful school media librarianship. Reference services begin with an effective and productive interview. The physical setting is a distinct part of the interview, and should be carefully planned in order to provide for optimum communications between the school library media specialist and the student.

You—The School Library Media Specialist

To conduct an appropriate and effective reference interview, specialized skills are required. Some of these skills are tangible—can be taught, practiced, and learned. However, some skills are intangible—your individualism or unique personality. Both tangible and intangible skills combine to create purposeful and interesting communications between the school library media specialist and the student, and hopefully, a successful reference interview.

Each school library media specialist has a badge of individuality that makes him or her unique—the librarian's style. Style, an intangible feature, is a combination of attitudes, appearances, and experiences—a myriad of special characteristics. As indefinable as style is, it plays a significant role in the reference interview. Success, still another intangible feature of the reference interview, is often overlooked as a school library media specialist. Many successful interviews conclude without the student actually finding the necessary information. This may occur because the information does not exist, the school library media center(s) cannot provide the information, or even because the student did not require information in the first place. Regardless, a successful reference interview is one in which the student feels satisfied that the school library media specialist has given personal attention and accurate information.

In addition to the intangible components, there are tangible skills that can be identified and practiced as a school library media specialist: nonverbal and verbal communications and skills. Nonverbal communications assist the school library media specialist in being approachable and interacting positively with students. These skills, in many instances, are already a part of the style or demeanor of the school library media specialist. Nonverbal skills are many times the easiest to learn and remember. They consist of the following: physical gestures, posture, facial expressions, tone of voice, and eye contact.

Verbal communications involve what is said as well as what is heard and understood by both the student and the school library media specialist. Verbal skills are often more difficult to isolate and master. Once a verbal skill is learned, it should be reviewed and refined in order to communicate more effectively. Verbal skills essential when conducting the reference interview include the following: positive (respectful) responses, motivational words (encouragers), verbal reflection, positive reactions, avoiding premature answers, diagnoses (or opinions), restating or paraphrasing content, remembering, open questions, and closure. Of primary importance throughout the interviewing procedure is careful listening and response. Talk to the students as if they are important (which they are) and welcomed (which they should be); take all questions seriously. Remember that appearance of attentiveness is also essential for effective communications. In addition, it is crucial that the school library media specialist possesses a genuinely helpful attitude and commitment to growth and the pursuit of knowledge.

Familiarity with the library collection and conducting an appropriate search for information may be thought of as a reference skill separate from the interview. It is, however, a critical step in the procedure and an important part of the reference interview process. Without knowledge of the library media center collection, the interview cannot continue; the question cannot be answered. *Empowering Learners* defines one role of the school library media specialist as information specialist. This role requires that the school library media specialist subscribe to various listservs or other forms of networking so they may provide the most up-to-date information on available resources both print and nonprint best suited for their students.

As a school library media specialist, knowledge of the resources—general, reference, and community—creates the context in which the student can ask further questions, as well as locate the desired information. The reference interview process relies on the complete skills of the school library media specialist, including expertise with all the library resources available, to provide the most accurate and complete response, and ultimately, information.

Questions and Questioning

Talk is the very basis of a reference interview, and school librarians should deliberately assure that the patron does the majority of talking and a great deal of the deciding of what will be talked about. Genuine listening is hard work and requires that the school library media specialist be alert to all verbal and nonverbal cues that transpire. Interviewing involves the hearing of the way things are being said, the tones used, and the expressions and gestures employed. Defining what is being asked and how to negotiate it is at the heart of the questioning process. Successful questioning requires active listening. This involves paying close attention to all that the student is saying. As a school library media specialist, you must become involved in the communications process; ascertain what the student wants to know.

Three basic purposes of reference interview questioning are as follows:

1) To ascertain what information the student wants.
2) To clarify the question (what it really means).
3) To discover the amount, level, and difficulty of the resources that will answer the question.

These purposes require the school library media specialist to carry on a conversation and to have time for such a dialogue. During the questioning procedure, it is important for the school library media specialist to:

- Determine why the question is being asked.
- Determine the subject of the question.
- Determine what the student has already discovered about the question (prior to asking).
- Determine what information is required to answer the question—the amount and format.
- Determine the barriers involved in answering the question (time, available resources, and so forth).
- Determine the most efficient and effective search strategy.

It is significant to understand that there are two major types of questions, open and closed. Open questions require the student to describe the need and its context. These questions frequently begin with what, where, and how. Open questions encourage further discussion. Closed questions, on the other hand, typically require the student to answer with either-or. These questions usually involve a prior-made judgment by the school library media specialist. Open and closed questions will often intermingle in the course of the reference interview. Once questioning is established, the subsequent search for information proceeds. The school library media specialist should ascertain from the student not only the information desired, but also exactly when the information is needed and in what format. At that point, the reference interview differs from other types of library situations. As a school library media specialist, it is imperative to foster research and information literacy skills with the student. You should, in most instances, allow the student to conduct the search, locate the information, and—to the best of his or her ability—become an independent learner. To paraphrase a portion of Information Power's Information Literacy Standards for Student Learning, the information literate student should:

- Access information efficiently and effectively
- Evaluate information critically and completely
- Use information accurately and completely

The successful interviewing techniques performed by the school library media specialist should lead the student to appropriate and accurate resources and foster the student's information literacy skills for socially responsible, lifelong learning.

A successful reference interview, using the most skilled questioning techniques, may not conclude with the complete achievement of the student's information needs (full and precise answer). However, if the student feels satisfied that he or she has been given adequate attention and has been directed to accurate resources, the interview was, indeed, a success.

Types of Reference Interviews

Not only does the school library media specialist need to ask appropriate questions, but must also make efficient use of time. By understanding the basic types of interviews used in school library media centers, this is made more plausible. The three most common types of reference interviews in the school library media center are: ready-reference, research projects, and readers' advisory.

Ready-reference interviews include questions that can be answered with short and factual information. These questions typically require the use of basic resources such as directories, encyclopedias, almanacs, dictionaries, and handbooks (both print and nonprint). The goal in ready-reference is to provide brief and accurate information in a short period of time.

Research project interviews lie at the other end of the spectrum. These questions involve in-depth coverage of a topic, often requiring the use of multiple sources of information. Research project questions may necessitate several interactions with the student over a period of time to achieve the desired results. As a school library media specialist, your goal is to provide the student with the most adequate materials, then to explain and encourage information literacy skills by the student.

Readers' advisory interviews basically take the form of recommending good leisure reading. As a school library media specialist, you must identify what the student considers good, as well as select the most appropriate materials for him or her. Of course, this is only possible with a current and adequate knowledge of the collection in your library media center, as well as a general knowledge of your school community. When conducting readers' advisory interviews, questions that might be asked of the student include, "What do you enjoy reading?" "What do you not like to read?" "Do you enjoy reading long books or short stories?" "Do you prefer reading a particular genre?" "Do you have a favorite author?" For younger students, showing them a variety of books may be helpful, allowing them time to preview the materials. It is also best to offer several choices. In addition, it is always beneficial, if possible, to provide a brief summary of the book or a booktalk.

Previously described in much literature, as a different type of reference interview, are electronic searches. Electronic searches now intermingle with other types of interviews. Many, if not most, searches will require online information. Therefore, a major goal as a school library media specialist is to locate the appropriate software and technologies, to assist the student with proper searching procedures and techniques. Additionally, it is extremely critical that the school library media specialist assists with proper evaluation of the electronic information. Accuracy and validity of the information retrieved electronically is crucial, still another role in the reference interview process.

Conclusion

The reference interview is an essential role as a school library media specialist. With the advent of new technologies in the school library media center, you are forced into a new pattern of service and a new approach to reference interviewing. However, the basics of reference services and questioning remain unchanged. The reference interview still involves human relations, communications, and interaction with the student. Good judgment and exceptional knowledge of resources remains imperative. The reference interview, in the past, present, and future, connects knowledge with students' information needs.

PART 4

Reference
and
the Web

Chapter 10

The Web in Today's Reference Services

Introduction

Essentially every aspect of school library media services has altered over the past few decades due to the emergence of new and innovative technologies. Reference skills, sources, and services are just one area that has changed to meet the needs of students in the diverse, global society of today. The Web has become the most important reference tool in the digital age, providing many of the electronic information sources required for reference services such as dictionaries and encyclopedias, informational Web sites, and search engines used for ready-reference and inquiry learning activities. This chapter discusses the Web and how its existence affects many aspects of reference sources and services for school libraries. It also illustrates how school librarians must work with students to use Web resources to meet instructional needs.

The day of seeking answers has not ended; only the process has changed. Accessing electronic information has two basic dimensions that distinguish it from print materials. The first is an almost unlimited storage capacity that continually expands. The second aspect is the ability to select from an enormous assemblage of data only what is needed. Mass storage and specific retrieval are both a blessing and a curse. The blessing is evident, but consider the curse. A mass of undifferentiated, many times unreliable, information is stored on the Web, which means that there may be thousands—even millions—of citations for any given topic. The problem is finding ways to discover the optimal information from among the heaps of data. It is the role of the school librarian to be the trained magician with the ability to extract (or assist the student in extracting) the desired data to meet specific informational needs. Today, students certainly have access to more information, but this does not necessarily mean that they have more knowledge. Is anyone the wiser because of the availability of limitless information?

The profusion of electronic resources available on the Internet has made finding information as simple as typing a phrase into a search engine and scanning the list of results. The information issue today is not related to access or quantity. It's more a matter of being able to effectively navigate the sea of information to obtain desired answers from authoritative sources. This issue is referred to as the *recall/precision problem*. For example, electronic search engines such as Google yield high recall and low precision results with keyword searches, while library catalogs or periodical databases that employ controlled subject terms are more likely to yield low recall and high precision results. It is important to think strategically about which electronic information resource to use for a particular information need because each one provides different kinds of information and involves different types of search strategies. The table below lists the common electronic information resources and tools available, the best match for the information need, how it ranks on the recall/precision issue, and the authoritativeness of the results.

Search Engines

The Web offers numerous added avenues and methods of searching. Instead of depending on assigned subject headings, one may use a wide variety of different approaches to gain the needed information. With the availability of the Web, the speed of searching has increased. However, speedy and accurate searches are only possible if the school librarian (and hence, the student) is knowledgeable about the effective and efficient use of the Internet search engines.

Search engines are essentially automated indexing programs that continuously gather information from the ever-expanding Internet and incorporate new information into their searchable databases. When a user has a question or "query," they are searching these massive index files for matching information. Search engines allow the user to enter keywords or phrases relating to a topic and retrieve information about Internet sites. Remember that all search engines have rules for formulating queries and often use specific symbols such as quotation marks and plus or minus symbols. Different search engines use different rules, which are often explained in the "help" or "advanced search" areas.

Everyone has had the experience of typing a word or phrase into a search engine and getting a million results, few of which are of any use. This is because most search interfaces used for retrieving electronic information sources use "keyword" as the default search setting, which ultimately leads to high recall and low precision results. Search engines often include other options for searching through different fields such as author, date, or subject headings, special codes that allow users to narrow or expand their searches, and advanced search pages, which provide users with a number of ways to narrow or expand their searches. Information on these features is typically found on the search engine's "help" or "advanced search" sections. The table below summarizes the types of search engines found on the Internet, the resources they index, and common search features. More detailed information about search engines can be found

Table 10.1: Matching Information Sources and Tools with Information Needs

Information Sources/ Tools and Examples	Information Need	Information Results
Web sites www.cnn.com www.worldbank.org	Electronic ready-reference, information inquiry, numerical data, pictures, videos	High recall/low precision; authority of sources are variable
Digital libraries books.google.com memory.loc.gov	Information inquiry, primary source information from electronic sources	Low recall/high precision; many digital libraries do not contain all items in full text; authoritative sources, but should be evaluated
Periodical databases www.ebscohost.com www.proquest.com www.abc-clio.com	Information inquiry related to current events cited in magazines, journals, newspapers available electronically	Low recall/high precision; some databases are indexes and do not contain full-text articles; authoritative sources, but should be evaluated
Virtual reference sites http://www.ipl.org	Electronic ready-reference from online dictionaries, encyclopedias, atlases, etc.	Low recall/high precision; authoritative sources, but should be evaluated
OPACs (Online Public Access Catalogs) worldcat.org	Information inquiry primarily from print sources or e-books	Low recall/high precision; most OPACs are indexes
Web 2.0 tools Wikipedia.org www.scientific american.com/podcast/	Information inquiry related to specialized information or current events in multimedia formats such as wikis, blogs, or pod/vod casts	High recall/low precision; authority must be carefully evaluated because content is often created by users and not vetted
Search engines www.google.com	Electronic ready-reference, information inquiry	High recall/low precision; search engines contain only information links and abstracts; all results must be carefully evaluated

Table 10.2: Common Features of Search Engines

Information Tool	Information Resource	Search Engine Features
Web search engines	Web sites	Keyword Phrase searching using " " Expansion using * or ? Exclude terms using - Exclude synonyms using + Advanced search functions
Digital libraries	Electronic books, full text, book excerpts, e-zines, magazines	Keyword Phrase searching Subject, author, title search Advanced search functions
Periodical databases	Electronic books, magazines, journal articles	Keyword Phrase searching using " " Subject, author, title search Advanced search functions
Online reference	Almanacs, dictionaries, etc.	Keyword Phrase searching Other functions depending on the resource
Library OPACS	Books, e-books, audiovisual, special collections	Keyword Phrase searching Author, title, subject search Advanced search functions
Web 2.0 sources	Blogs, pod/vod casts, wikis, etc.	Keyword Other functions depending on the resource

on sites such as Webreference (http://webreference.com/content/search) and Search Engine Watch (http://searchenginewatch.com). You will find that every person searches for information differently and has favorite resources, whether they are print, nonprint, or Web sites. Good searching begins well before one enters the topic terms (keywords) into a search engine. Critical thinking capabilities are as necessary in using a search engine as they are in using any print resource or database. Searching the Web requires part skill, and a little bit of art.

Electronic Resources, Searching Strategies, and Tips

Each type of electronic resource, such as an online encyclopedia, library catalog, or Web site, typically has a search engine associated with it. For example, Web sites are found through search engines such as Google and Yahoo, while online periodicals are found through the search interfaces associated with online periodical databases. In general, high precision recall from electronic searches depends on how well users understand the source they are using to find information and the quality of their search query. Users who understand which information sources are best to use to meet particular information needs, who understand the particularities of each search engine, and who are able to develop a well-formed search query will be successful users of information and ideas in the 21st century. As a school librarian who guides students through the information search process, consider the following suggestions when assisting students with their information needs:

- Anticipate students' information needs through formal and informal collaborative planning.
- For common information needs consider developing a virtual reference collection for your media center containing links to online reference tools and digital libraries, and pathfinders for information inquiry assignments.
- Prior to their search, help students define and refine their information questions in order to choose the appropriate electronic source.
- Reduce ineffective searching by choosing the correct electronic resource and search terminology for the information need, and review functions of the search tool with students before they begin.
- Model effective search strategies for users, but do not do the work for them.

Evaluating Electronic Resources

A Web resource may be different from a print source, but it remains essentially the same in purpose and scope. Web materials can make steps easier, considerably more efficient, and certainly more comprehensive. However, each resource must be evaluated for authority and appropriateness for the question at hand. Sometimes it is quicker to use a print resource to find an authoritative answer than using a Web site found using a search engine. It is vital to know when to turn to print resources, when to use the Web, and when to avoid them all in favor of consulting an expert in the field. The bottom line is that correct information must be located for students in the most efficient and effective manner possible. Similar criteria are used to evaluate Web sites.

Figure 10.1: Exercise: Search Engines

EXERCISE: EVALUATING SEARCH ENGINES

This exercise will help you understand the different searching functions of commonly used search engines.

Ask the following questions as you explore the four search engines listed below:

- Does it include links to detailed help?

- How large is it?

- What type of searching does it use?

- How does it search proper names?

- Does it have advanced searching?

- What search options are available to narrow your search?

- What search options are available to broaden your search?

- Does it collect information about your searches?

    Google: www.google.com

    Bing: www.bing.com

    Yahoo: www.yahoo.com

    Ask: www.ask.com

Which one do you like the best? Why?

Which one do you like least? Why?

From *Reference Skills for the School Librarian: Tools and Tops, Third Edition* by Ann Marlow Riedling, Loretta Shake, and Cynthia Houston. Santa Barbara, CA: Linworth. Copyright © 2013.

The definition of an authoritative resource is a slippery matter. Authority is not confined to particular formats such as newspapers, books, or journals. Authority typically means that the item has been reviewed by a group of peers and the information contained in the item is correct. Furthermore, even though resources such as newspapers may be considered authoritative, they may not represent a balanced point of view (e.g., *Forbes* vs. *Mother Jones*). Information-literate students understand how to evaluate sources for authority and bias using specific criteria. This ability is called *information fluency* and involves the following skills: determining the accuracy, credibility, and relevance of a source; distinguishing among facts, points of view, and opinions presented in a source; and selecting the most useful resources for a particular information need.

Evaluation criteria for print resources—including accuracy, authority, bias, arrangement, presentation, and cost—can be applied to evaluating electronic information sources. With electronic information resources, authority is one of the most critical criteria to consider. When considering the authority of a Web page it is important that the following questions be asked in order to identify who created the information source and if their biases skew the presentation of information:

- Is the creator an individual or an institution?
- Does the information source list the authors' or institutions' affiliation so that any potential bias can be determined?
- Is this information easy to find or hidden?
- What are the credentials of the author/s and how is their credibility established?
- Is credibility established through education or affiliation?
- Is there information on how to contact the author/s?
- How is the reputation of the organization established?
- Is the organization a business, government agency, nonprofit organization?
- Does the information item contain any advertising that might bias the information?
- Does the information present multiple points of view through a variety of information sources?

Good sources of information for evaluating electronic resources can be found at the following sites:

Cornell University Library
        http://www.library.cornell.edu/olinuris/ref/research/skill26.htm

Kathy Schrock's Guide for Educators
        http://school.discoveryeducation.com/schrockguide/eval.html

Western Kentucky University Libraries
        http://www.wku.edu/library/dlps/infolit/

School Library Reference Services in the Digital Age

The Web is the most important change in electronic information reference services since the development of electronic resources themselves. The greatest contribution of the Internet is not the technology, as impressive as it may be, but the sense of connection it makes possible between individuals and groups. The Internet is not really a source of information, but rather a means of communication—the "ultimate" communication network. With regard to reference services for school libraries, the World Wide Web is all about providing information. As it grows and continues to change as a forum for the exchange of information, school librarians must remain actively involved. As explained in *Empowering Learners*, "The development of social technology tools has created an interconnected global society where learning, social, and work environments have moved across physical boundaries. . . . To successfully navigate through these fluid boundaries, learners must embody the characteristics of global citizenship and be skilled users of information technologies" (AASL, 2009, 7). The Web is so vast that knowing all of what is available is literally impossible; it is growing and developing in many directions simultaneously. The nonhierarchical nature of the Internet can be a challenge and an opportunity for school librarians and students. The Internet links thousands of other communication and data networks with one another and with individual users. The lack of standardization, however, requires school librarians to invest a great deal of time and energy in learning which resources are of most importance to the library and student population. It is a certainty that standardization of terminology and resource formats will become more widespread in the years ahead. As a school librarian, you must assist students to effectively and efficiently use the Web, create a culture of information inquiry, and create information-fluent students (those who can access, evaluate, organize, and use electronic information) for tomorrow's world.

As time progresses, there will be numerous potential roles available for school librarians—it takes imagination, ingenuity, and much hard work. Success does not come easily. As school librarians, we must embrace the continual changes, not resist them. We must move forward to make the school libraries of tomorrow purposeful and exciting. We must make information gathering effective and efficient—and create information-literate, socially responsible, lifelong learners. The rewards will be widespread. As the well-known metaphor states, opportunities are like sunrises. If you miss them they are gone. So is the case with technologies in the world of reference sources and services for school librarians.

One common misconception is that in the future there will be less dependence on the physical library media center. Why is this concept not true? Information needs are growing and becoming more complex. The result is that there will be an increased need for experts, school librarians with skills in searching, accessing, using, and evaluating information efficiently and effectively. In addition, students will now, more than ever before, need to be taught information literacy skills. Because information sources have expanded far beyond a library's physical walls, media centers are no longer viewed as the sole source of information for students' learning needs. However, because 21st-century learner standards require students to be fluent in critical inquiry and decision-making skills, the media center plays a central role in providing resources and instruction for 21st-century learning. Who better to teach them than the school librarian?

In response to changes in information resources and the needs of 21st-century learners, many libraries are moving to a new model for information sources and services called the Learning Commons model. The Learning Commons model envisions libraries as information hubs supporting learners by providing library resources, technology tools and support, tutoring, and other academic support services, all in one central location. This model is a learner-centered and service-based model rather than an organization-based administrative model. This model requires a shift in thinking of the school media center as entirely a fixed and physical entity filled with items that must be managed, to a flexible and shared physical and virtual space filled with users engaged in a variety of social and educational activities. The role of the school librarian in a Learning Commons is transformed from "keeper of the books" to a program director with specialized knowledge in information sources and services who coordinates the use of a dynamic space shared by all members of the learning community. Because educational technology has become flexible, portable, and interoperable, the computer lab can also be a shared and flexible resource managed by the Learning Commons team (Loertscher, Koechlin, and Zwaan, 2011).

In the Learning Commons model, the media center plays multiple roles. According to the *Partnership for 21st Century Skills*, the school media center not only carries out its traditional role of bringing information resources to learners, but also provides the tools and infrastructure that enable learners to analyze, synthesize, and evaluate resources in ways that demonstrate learning and create new knowledge. It must offer places for formal learning in which large groups can gather for presentations; places for social learning where teams can collaborate on projects; and places for individual learning where individuals can find a quiet space for reading, reflection, or relaxation. These centers must also connect kids and adults to the wider world beyond the school by providing the audio and video communications technologies that build bridges between people and places all over the globe. According to Loertscher, Koechlin, and Zwaan (2011), in a school Learning Commons, the following characteristics are typically present:

- A large, caring, comfortable and flexible learning environment
- On-demand physical and virtual access to materials, information, and guidance
- Supportive assistance from knowledgeable adults and peers
- Shared decision making regarding use of space and resources
- Technology and resources for project-based and inquiry learning activities
- Programs and activities involving the entire school

For the learner, the Learning Commons is a place for them to engage in inquiry activities with guidance from information specialists. For the teacher, the Learning Commons supports the higher-level thinking, technology-integration learning activities they are engaging in with their students. A key component of the Learning Commons model is the notion that information sources and services provided by the media center be available outside the library walls and the traditional school day. Providing information resources and assistance virtually is important for students who are completing projects and homework assignments from home after school hours. Virtual information services can assume a variety of forms and formats depending on the resources available and the information needs of the school. Schools that currently offer virtual information services to teachers and students typically include the following resources:

- Web-based library catalog for searching print materials
- Web-based periodical databases for accessing magazines and journal articles
- Virtual information pages for specific topics and assignments in the forms of Pathfinders, WebQuests, Bibliographies, or Wikis

As long as students require information and guidance in becoming effective users of information and ideas, there will be a need for school librarians and school libraries. As the school information specialist and expert in 21st-century learning models and technologies, the media specialist is responsible to ensure that the media center is proactive in meeting the needs of 21st-century learners. Now and in the future there will be significant changes to the roles and resources of the media center in the school educational program. The previous model discussed the transformation of media centers into learner-centered Learning Commons. Making the transition to a space dominated by flexible seating arrangements for individual and group inquiry leads one to consider the fate of the traditional library stacks and ultimately to the future of the print reference collection. For examples, if students need to look up a word or topic in a dictionary or encyclopedia, it would be much easier for them to access digital resources from their wireless laptops or phones than it would be to walk to the reference section and select the item from the shelf. In the past several years, as reference tools such as encyclopedias, almanacs, and periodical guides have become available in electronic format, the reference section in school media centers has been shrinking. The cost of maintaining current volumes of encyclopedias and almanacs is high, and most states now share the costs of providing these resources electronically. Without a doubt, the future of information services in 21st-century school libraries will be predominately delivered electronically and involve the school librarian in guiding students in locating and using these materials independently rather than directing them to a location on the library shelf.

The challenges for school librarians are to anticipate the changes taking place in education and information services and to manage the resources of the school library to stay ahead of these changes. According to library architect Rolf Erikson, the 21st-century school library must look beyond tradition to the future, to what is needed to help fulfill the educational mission, goals, and objectives of the school. Traditional library environments are primarily text based, require learning the system from experts (librarians), and are constructed for individual use. This traditional model is no longer appropriate. These sentiments are especially true for the traditional reference section in the school media center. Below are some important challenges media specialists face in transforming the reference section for the 21st-century media center.

Balancing Print and Electronic Reference Resources

It is clear that as electronic reference resources become increasingly available, print reference resources will decrease. Media specialists will need to conduct patron surveys and collection analysis to determine which reference resources are useful in print format, which are useful in electronic format, and which resources should be maintained in both print and electronic formats.

Changing the Size and Focus of the Media Center Reference Collection

In the 21st century what will be the size, focus, and composition of the media center reference area? It is clear that students must have access to electronic information resources for their information needs, so the 21st-century reference center must include computer access. The number of print reference materials will certainly decrease in size, and as general reference moves online, specialized reference tools, such as *Atlas of the Oceans*, may move onto the shelves.

Transforming the Reference Shelf into a 21st-Century Exploratorium

The original purpose of the reference section was to provide users with easy-to-use, authoritative resources providing a general introduction to a particular topic. Online reference tools generally meet the immediate information needs of users, so the reference area must be transformed into a center for social interaction, individual and group exploration, and guidance in the location, access, and use of information resources.

With these thoughts in mind, transforming the reference section of the library into a 21st-century learning space will include developing easy access to technology, inviting spaces for social interaction, and spaces for individual inquiry. But it remains to be seen exactly what the future will hold.

As school libraries are transformed more and more into a learning commons, with multipurpose spaces and media in multiple formats, the reference and information services function will become increasingly important. To provide information services to students in a service-oriented culture, school librarians must make use of the 21st-century information tools and Web 2.0 communication resources to maintain contact with library users. Web 2.0 tools have the potential to bring the media center to where students are interacting with electronic information and should be considered a part of the information services plan of the school media center. WebTools4U2Use (http://webtools4u2use.wikispaces.com/) is a Wiki space for media specialists who are interested in using Web 2.0 tools for information services. The site suggests the following five Web 2.0 tools to try out in the media center for expanding information services outside the library walls:

- Wikis—Encyclopedic Web sites that media specialists can maintain to direct students to important information resources related to school assignments and projects
- Blogs—Online journals media specialists can maintain to keep users interested in information services in the library
- Photo/video sharing sites—Web sites containing photos and videos users upload and share with others
- RSS feeds—Method for informing your users about updates to your information services
- Facebook/MySpace/Twitter—Social networking tools students regularly use to maintain their social networks and communicate with each other
- Podcasts—A convenient way to integrate audio information about library activities into the lives of students who subscribe to this service

Useful Web Sites

Cornell University Library Critically Analyzing Information Sources
>   http://www.library.cornell.edu/olinuris/ref/research/skill26.htm
>   *Thorough discussion of how to analyze information sources, including evaluation criteria.*

Dig the Library
>   http://www.digthelibrary.com
>   *Hundreds of online resources for the K–12 community reviewed and evaluated by teachers.*

Digital Information Fluency
>   http://21cif.com
>   *Professional development and tools for teachers in support of 21st-century information fluency.*

Evaluating Web Sources
>   http://library.queensu.ca/inforef/tutorials/qcat/evalint.htm
>   *Site considering questions to assist in evaluation of Web resources.*

Information Quality WWW Virtual Library
>   http://www.ciolek.com/WWWVL-InfoQuality.html
>   *Site offering resources and criteria for evaluating electronic information resources.*

Kathy Schrock's Guide for Educators
>   http://school.discoveryeducation.com/schrockguide/eval.html
>   *Resources for teachers and students on how to evaluate Internet resources.*

Reference Materials Collections
>   www.cln.org/subjects/refmat.html
>   *Web site offering numerous links related to reference materials, divided into "general reference materials" and "specific reference tools."*

Resources for School Librarians
>   http://www.sldirectory.com
>   *Includes such areas as Learning and Teaching, Information Access, Program Administration, Technology, Education and Employment, and Continuing Education.*

Virtual Salt: World Wide Web Research Tools
>   http://www.virtualsalt.com/search.htm
>   *A useful Web site divided into Search Engines, Directories, and so on.*

WebTools4u2Use.

>http://webtools4u2use.wikispaces.com/
>*Comprehensive listing and review of Web 2.0 tools for schools and libraries.*

Western Kentucky University Libraries Information Literacy

>http://www.wku.edu/library/dlps/infolit/
>*Tutorials, guides, and references for information literacy.*

World Wide School Library

>www.worldwideschool.org/library/catalogs/bysubject-top.html
>*An excellent resource, divided by subject, title, and author.*

PART 5

Scenarios and Exercises for School Librarians

Introduction

It has been said that experience is the best teacher. With that in mind, the following chapter is presented to offer the next best thing, an aid in the form of Reference Scenarios and Exercises.

Three primary categories of reference for school librarians are as follows:

1) Readers'/Information Service
2) Selection and Evaluation of Reference Materials
3) User Instruction

Readers'/Information Service involves extremely delicate forms of assistance. As a school librarian, you are in the position of crossing a very thin line between reference and readers' service, which accounts for your answering such questions as: What is a good book on 9/11? What is the best novel to read? Will you give me the scariest book you have in the library? Will you find a book about sex education (for a friend)? To complicate matters even further, the school librarian is also involved with confidentiality and censorship issues. This all-encompassing area is diverse and complicated for the school librarian.

Selection and Evaluation of Reference Materials is a highly individualized process for the school librarian. No two school librarians will approach these processes in precisely the same manner. However, one universal, critical rule when considering the selection and evaluation of resources for your media center is knowledge of the needs (both known and anticipated) of your users. In addition, as a school librarian, you must consider not only the user (student), but also the community, administration, parents, teachers, and staff with whom you work. It is a complex and extremely significant job.

Unlike User Instruction in public and academic libraries, User Instruction for students is an essential component of the school library media center. School librarians do not have the luxury of not providing proper and complete training regarding the basic sources and services of the library media center, including the effective teaching of library skills and information literacy. Indeed, it is time consuming; however, without it little time is available for other services.

In light of these three categories, the following chapter is intended to provide the prospective (or even the experienced) school librarian with insight into the numerous situations that may arise in a library media center. The scenarios and exercises are designed to provide the school librarian with a glimpse into the world of reference services. This chapter encompasses both large and small library media centers, and urban and rural settings. The situations include both practical and philosophical aspects of reference services for school librarians. The scenarios and exercises are to be read thoughtfully, pondered, and, hopefully, discussed with other prospective or experienced school librarians. The exercises provide useful guidelines for teaching reference skills; they can be accomplished individually or as a group. Following each scenario, a list of questions is supplied for you to consider and reflect upon. As there is no one correct solution for the scenarios, answers are not provided. Expectantly, attentive conversation will arise from the readings, discussions that will search the very heart of reference services for school librarians.

Special Notes for Instructors

The following scenarios and exercises are provided as a means of eliciting discussion and spurring thoughtful conversation with and among prospective school librarians in the university or college classroom setting. As the instructor of the course, your mission is to guide discussion, as well as creative and critical thinking, based on the knowledge, experiences, and insights that you possess. These are simply tools to encourage more in-depth thought regarding specific reference processes and services. They could also be used to guide student discussion in Web-enhanced or Web-based courses. In addition, technologies could be used to encourage the discussions. For instance, students could e-mail other classmates and experienced school librarians about the situations and exercises prior to in-class discussions. Adequate, appropriate, and creative discussion will only occur with your expert guidance and direction.

Although some of the questions for each scenario or exercise can be answered with a rather simple response, deeper conversations can occur by providing probing questions. The following are examples of such questions: "Why or why not?" "What if?" "What might happen if?" "Are there alternatives; if so, what are they?" "Can you give another example?" "What ideas can you add to this?" "Why is this significant?" "Do you agree or disagree; why or why not?" "Will you elaborate and explain further?" "What would you do, and why?" "What specific documents could be used to assist in this situation or exercise?" "Are there more ways than one to solve this problem; what are they?" "Have you observed this situation actually occurring; how was it handled?" "How might the answer alter due to differences in school setting, administration, student population, and so forth?"

Do not remain confined to merely questions and answers. A variety of teaching methods or strategies can be helpful and valuable using scenarios or case situations. Examples of exercises for use in the classroom include:

- Role play.
- Think-Pair-Share: Provide student thinking time; then, allow discussion with a partner and presentation back to the entire class.
- Ask a student at random to summarize another person's point or response.
- Have students describe how they arrived at an answer.
- Play devil's advocate: Ask students to defend their reasoning against different points of view.
- Ask students to create their own questions or scenarios.
- Have students write their responses on paper. Pass these anonymous papers to other classmates and have them respond to each other's answers.

You, as the instructor, are the key to eliciting the desired discussions. The scenarios and exercises—and subsequent questions—initiate the process of thinking and planning regarding reference services for school library media centers. You are limited only by your creativity and imagination.

Chapter 11

Scenarios and Exercises

Scenario (Elementary School): Famous First Facts

Lafayette Elementary School recently received funding from a dedicated parent of a previous student. A large portion of the money was earmarked for the library media center. Mrs. Jean Noe, the school librarian, after thoughtful consideration purchased the online database Famous First Facts for her library media center. Jean is very excited about this purchase and realizes how much it can offer her students. However, although she has advertised this new purchase, students and teachers remain loyal to the Internet (for example, Google searches). Mrs. Noe wants to demonstrate to the teachers and students what a useful reference tool Famous First Facts is, but is not certain how to accomplish this task.

Questions:

1) How can an online database be more useful than the Internet?

2) What are the "good aspects" of an online database as opposed to the Internet?

3) List several ways teachers could incorporate the use of an online database into the curriculum. (Try a minimum of two curriculum areas.)

4) As a school librarian, describe precisely what you would do—step-by-step—to introduce this new purchase and entice students and teachers to use it in place of the Internet (when appropriate).

Exercise (Elementary School): Planning a Search

For this exercise, pretend that you are an elementary-aged student! Then choose one area that interests a K–5 student, such as dinosaurs, airplanes, cooking, drawing, and so forth. Complete the worksheet below. Remember, sometimes when we put things in "black and white," they become more real and you can stay focused (this is something useful to remind your students).

1) Write down your area of interest and make it into a question. (For example, how do airplanes fly?) Use the Super3 (Plan, Do, Review) model from chapter 1 to organize your activities.

2) Go to the school library media center and locate (and read) four reference resources that help you answer the question. (For example, an online encyclopedia, a Pathfinder, a book, and a person.)

3) Summarize the information you found. Put the pieces of information together; organize them such that you have a one-page paper that answers your question.

4) Present your paper in class using the Super3 model as a structure and obtain feedback from your classmates.

5) Discuss what you would do differently or the same the next time you needed to conduct research.

Sometimes it is helpful to look at things from the student's side, to provide more helpful references sources and services.

Scenario (Middle School): Evaluation of Electronic Information

The Glovett Middle School, a wealthy independent school located in the southeastern portion of the United States, is blessed with all of the latest technologies and resources. Mr. Ken Westley has served as the school librarian for the past two years; he tries his best to assist all of his patrons effectively and efficiently. Students at Glovett Middle visit the library media center frequently with their classes, as well as independently. Unfortunately, however, the majority of research performed by students appears to be via the Internet.

Ken wants the students and teachers to use a variety of reference tools, but does not know how to accomplish this task. He has numerous reference materials, print and electronic, and would like for all of them to be used appropriately.

Questions:
1) Why are some reference materials more efficient and effective than the Internet?

2) What measures could Ken take to assure the use of all reference sources?
   By teachers?
   By students?
   By administrators?

3) Describe specifically what you would do to employ the use of all types of reference sources. Be specific, taking it step-by-step. (Possibly a strategic plan?)

Exercise (Middle School): Online Databases

Pretend that you are a middle school student. Your school librarian asks you to do the following:

Visit your local school, public, or academic library. It is important to understand that every library purchases specific online indexes and databases. What they buy depends on the size of the library, the type of library, and what the librarian selects.

Now, access the online databases available. Explore them, go to various links, and learn how they work, what they provide, and so forth. (Remember, just as you learn more about driving a car by doing it rather than reading about it, it is much easier to learn about online indexes and abstracts if one explores and uses them!)

Answer the following questions regarding the online indexes and databases you explored:

1) What was the primary focus of each online database?

2) What is useful/useless about each online database visited? (Did it contain many pertinent articles? Was it user friendly?)

3) Can you search by author, title, keyword?

4) Does it include an advanced search?

5) Can you print the information or send it to an e-mail address?

6) On a scale of 1 to 10, how do you rate each online database?

Exercise (High School): Research Skills

The English teachers at Scribner High School have asked if you would teach research skills to their freshman English classes. They are particularly interested in students learning how to effectively evaluate Web sites. They also would like to be sure students are familiar with citing sources.

1) Evaluate the research models from chapter 1—which one would be best for high school students?

2) Visit www.radcab.com and discuss if this method for evaluating Web sites is appropriate for high school students. Are there other ways to evaluate Web sites? What are they?

3) Will you use a Web site to teach citing sources? Which one do you feel is most appropriate for high school?

4) Would this be an appropriate time to visit copyright? Boolean operators? School-owned online databases? Other online sources students have access to?

5) After the initial request for you to teach this lesson, is there a need to collaborate further with the teachers?

Exercise (High School): Bogus Web Sites

Not everything in black and white is true! As a school librarian, you must relay this information to your students. This (particularly) also applies to the World Wide Web. High school students must learn to evaluate Web sites in order to select reference materials that are valid, reliable, objective, and useful.

Pretend that you are a high school student. (This would be a great exercise for high school students to participate in!) For this exercise, view the following Web sites and answer the questions listed below for each site.

http://beefnutrition.org
http://www.dhmo.org/

1) Who is the author or creator of this site? Can you contact this person?

2) Is the author or creator qualified to write this work? How do you know? Does the author have any other publications? What are they?

3) What are the purpose, goals, and objectives of this Web site?

4) Why was this site produced?

5) Who published the site?

6) How detailed is the information?

7) Does the author or creator express opinions? If so, are they clearly labeled?

8) Does this Web site include advertising? If so, is that necessarily bad?

9) When was the Web site created? Is it obvious? Has it been updated?

10) What does this site offer that you cannot find elsewhere?

11) How current are the links? Are they useful? Are they easy to navigate?

12) Is there a balance between images and text?

13) Is the site free of spelling and grammatical errors?

Appendix

Publisher Information

ABC-CLIO
130 Cremona Drive
Santa Barbara, CA 93117
Phone: 805-968-1911
Toll Free: 800-368-6868
Fax: 800-685-9685
http://www.abc-clio.com

American Library Association
50 East Huron Street
Chicago, IL 60611
Toll Free: 800-545-2433
Fax: 312-944-2641
http://www.ala.org/

American Psychological Association
750 First Street NE
Washington, DC 20002-4242
Phone: 202-336-5500
http://www.apa.org/

Association of Educational
Communications and Technology (AECT)
1800 N. Stonelake Dr., Suite 2
Bloomington, IN 47404
Phone: 812-335-7675
Fax: 812-335-7678
http://www.aect.org/

Belknap Press/Harvard University
Press Reference Library
79 Garden Street
Cambridge, MA 02138
Toll Free: 800-448-2242
Fax: 800-962-4983
http://www.hup.harvard.edu/

Britannica
310 S. Michigan Ave.
Chicago, IL 60604
Toll Free: 800-621-3900
Fax: 800-344-9624
http://www.eb.com

Brodart
500 Arch Street
Williamsburg, PA 17705
Phone: 800-233-8467
Intl. Phone: 570-326-2461
Fax: 800-999-6799
http://www.brodart.com

Cambridge University Press
Edinburgh Building
Shaftesbury Road
Cambridge CB2 2RU
Phone: 44-0-1223-312393
Fax: 44-0-1223-315052
http://www.cup.cam.ac.uk/

Charles Scribner's Sons
University of South Carolina Press
718 Devine St.
Columbia, SC 29208
Toll Free: 800-768-2500
Fax: 800-868-0740
http://www.sc.edu/uscpress/

The College Board
45 Columbus Avenue
New York, NY 10023-6992
Phone: 212-713-8000
http://www.collegeboard.org/

Columbia University Press
61 West 62nd Street
New York, NY 10023
Phone: 212-459-0600
http://cup.columbia.edu/

Dorling Kindersley
3 Chandos Place
London WC2N 4HS
United Kingdom
Phone: 44-0-20-7753-7335
Fax: 44-0-20-7969-8027
http://www.dk.com/

EBSCO Publishing
10 Estes Street
Ipswich, MA 01938
Phone: 978-356-6500
Toll Free (USA & Canada): 800-758-5995
International: (access code) 800-3272-6000
Fax (Tech Support): 978-356-9372
Fax (Customer Service): 978-356-6565
http://www.ebsco.com/

Gale Cengage Learning
Toll Free: 800-877-GALE
Fax: 800-414-5043
http://www.gale.cengage.com/

Government Printing Office
732 North Capitol Street, NW
Washington, DC 20401-0001
Phone: 202-512-1800
Toll Free: 866-512-800
Fax: 202-512-2250
http://www.gpo.gov/

HarperCollins Publishers
10 East 53rd Street
New York, NY 10022
Phone: 212-207-7000
http://www.harpercollins.com/

Harvard University Press
79 Garden Street
Cambridge, MA 02138
Toll Free: 800-448-2242
Fax: 800-962-4983
http://www.hup.harvard.edu/

Horn Book
56 Roland Street, Suite 200
Boston, MA 02129
Toll Free: 800-325-1170
Fax: 617-628-0882
http://www.hbook.com/

Houghton Mifflin Harcourt
222 Berkeley Street
Boston, MA 02116
Phone: 617-351-5000
http://www.hmco.com/

Infobase Publishing
132 West 31st Street, 17th Floor
New York, NY 10001
Phone: 800-322-8755
Fax: 800-678-3633

Macmillan
175 Fifth Avenue
New York, NY 10010
Phone: 646-307-5151
htpp://us.macmillan.com

Merriam Webster
47 Federal Street
PO Box 281
Springfield, MA 01102
Phone: 413-734-3134
Fax: 413-731-5979
http://www.m-w.com/

Modern Language Association of America
26 Broadway, 3rd floor
New York, NY 10004-1789
Phone: 646-576-5000
Fax: 646-458-0030
http://www.mla.org

National Geographic Society
P.O. Box 11303
Des Moines, IA 50340
Toll Free: 800-437-5521
Fax: 515-362-3345
http://www.nationalgeographic.com

NewsBank
5801 Pelican Bay Boulevard, Suite 600
Naples, FL 34108
Toll Free: 800-243-7694
http://NewsBank.com/

Omnigraphics
P.O. Box 31-1640
Detroit, MI 48231
Toll Free: 800-234-1340
Fax: 800-875-1340
http://www.omnigraphics.com/

Orion Publishing Group
Orion House
5 Upper Saint Martin's Lane
London WC2H 9EA
UK
Phone: 020-7240-3444
Fax: 020-7240-4822

Oxford University Press
2001 Evans Road
Cary, NC 27513
Phone: 919-677-0977
http://www.oup-usa.org/

Prentice-Hall
One Lake Street
Upper Saddle River, NJ 07458
Phone: 201-236-7156
Toll Free: 800-382-3419
http://prenticehall.com/

Princeton University Press
41 William Street
Princeton, NJ 08540-5237
Phone: 609-258-4900
Fax: 609-258-6305
http://press.princeton.edu/

ProQuest LLC
789 E. Eisenhower Parkway
P.O. Box 1346
Ann Arbor, MI 48106-1346
Phone: 734-761-4700
http://www.ProQuest.com/

R. R. Bowker
630 Central Avenue
New Providence, NJ 07974
Phone: 908-286-0288
http://www.bowker.com/

Rand McNally
P.O. Box 7600
Chicago, IL 60680-7600
Toll Free: 800-275-7263
http://www.randmcnally.com/

Random House
1745 Broadway
New York, NY 10019
Phone: 212-782-9000
Fax: 212-302-7985
Toll Free: 800-726-0600
http://www.randomhouse.com/

Reed Elsevier
125 Park Avenue
23rd Floor
New York, NY 10017
Phone: 212-309-8100
http://www.reedelsevier.com/

Rowman & Littlefield Publishing Group
15200 NBN Way
PO Box 191
Blue Ridge Summit, PA 17214
Toll Free: 800-462-6420
https://rowman.com/

Salem Press
Two University Plaza, Suite 121
Hackensack, NJ 07601
Toll Free: 800-221-1592
Fax: 201-968-1411
http://www.salempress.com/

Simon & Schuster
100 Front Street
Riverside, NJ 08075
Toll Free: 800-331-6531
http://www.simonandschuster.com/

William Morrow
an imprint of HarperCollins Publishers
1350 Avenue of the Americas
New York, NY 10019
Phone: 212-473-1452
http://www.williammorrow.com/

World Book
233 N. Michigan Ave., Suite 2000
Chicago, IL 60601
Phone: 312-729-5800
Toll Free: 800-WORLDBK
Fax: 312-729-5600
http://www.worldbook.com/

World Resources Institute
10 G Street, NE, Suite 800
Washington, DC 20002
Phone: 202-729-7600
Fax: 202-729-7610
http://www.wri.org/

Glossary

AASL's *Empowering Learners*: This book of guidelines for the American Association of School Librarians (AASL) states that the library media program should provide, "a well-developed collection of books, periodicals, and non-print materials in a variety of formats that support curricular topics and are suited to inquiry learning and the user's needs and interests."

AECT: Association for Educational Communications and Technology

Almanacs, Yearbooks, and Handbooks: These types of reference sources provide factual information about alphabetic or classed order, giving address, affiliations, etc., for individuals, countries, governments, and statistical trends.

American Association of School Librarians (AASL): This organization developed the *Standards for the 21st-Century Learner* (2007) and *Standards for the 21st-Century Learner in Action* (2008), which address four main goals for learners:
1) Inquire, think critically, and gain knowledge.
2) Draw conclusions, make informed decisions, apply knowledge to new situations, and create new knowledge.
3) Share knowledge and participate ethically and productively as members of our democratic society.
4) Pursue personal and aesthetic growth.

Bibliographic Instruction: This term is defined as any activity that is designed to teach students how to locate and use information in the library, as well as sources that exist beyond the physical boundaries of the school library.

Big6 Model: This process describes the six thinking steps one goes through any time there is an information problem to be solved. It was developed by Eisenberg and Berkowitz.

Biographical Sources: These can be divided into several different types: national bibliographies, trade bibliographies, library catalogs, union catalogs, and subject catalogs.

Blog: A Web site containing the writer's or group of writers' own experiences, observations, opinions, etc., and often having images and links to other Web sites.

Cognitive Development: The process of acquiring intelligence and increasingly advanced thought and problem-solving ability from infancy to adulthood.

Common Core Standards (CCS): To date, 45 of the 50 states have adopted the Common Core Standards (CCS), which currently outlines the P–12 curriculum for English Language Arts, Literacy in History/Social Studies, and Science and Technical Subjects.

Critical Thinking: This term refers to disciplined thinking that is clear, rational, open-minded, and informed by evidence.

Digital Divide: This is now a generational term, and refers to the differences between the ways people born before 1977 regard access to information compared with those born after 1977.

Directories: A list of persons or organizations, systematically arranged, usually in numerous items, such as people, organizations, things, current and historical events, and other features.

Empowering Learners: Guidelines for School Library Media Programs: A title that states, "The school librarian collaborates with the teaching staff to develop an up-to-date collection of print and digital resources in multiple genres that can this be combined with the first entry" (AASL, 2009). It appeals to differences in age, gender, ethnicity, reading abilities, and information needs."

Factbooks: General reference tools providing basic facts on particular topics such as countries, sports, or time periods.

Gazetteers: Composed of a list of geographical names and/or physical features. It is a geographical dictionary for finding lists of cities, mountains, rivers, and populations.

Geographical Index: An alphabetical list of all place-names that appear on the map.

Handbooks: These are sometimes called manuals; they serve as guides to a particular subject.

Historical Atlases: These are necessary for the study of early exploration, boundary changes, and military campaigns.

Imposed vs. Unimposed Queries: Queries are another word for questions. Imposed means put, place, presume, prescribe, introduce, institute, or fix. Unimposed is the opposite of imposed.

Indexes: Whether these are separate guides to periodical articles or part of books, they are used to reveal specific portions of information in a larger unit.

Information Literacy: The American Library Association's (ALA) Presidential Committee on Information Literacy, Final Report, states, "To be information literate, a person must be able to recognize when information is needed and has the ability to locate, evaluate, and use effectively the needed information." Information literacy is important to all libraries, library users, and the general public.

Information Seeking Process: This model conceptualizes the construction of meaning through active participation with information resources. It encourages an in-depth focus that enables students to seek more relevant information and produce a product of higher quality. This process was developed by Carol Kuhlthau.

Interdisciplinary: Combining or involving two or more academic disciplines or fields of study.

Literary Criticism: A written evaluation of a work of literature; the informed analysis and evaluation of literature.

Literacy Development: Best practices for teaching reading to achieve student success.

National Governors' Association: This association has led a nationwide initiative to provide a clear and consistent curriculum framework for what students should know and be able to do to be prepared for college and work. This is now known as the *Common Core Standards*.

Online Periodical Databases: This can be best described as an online collection of information that is organized into records that can be searched. Databases are used for almost everything from finance to home address books.

Online Periodical Indexes: Indexes that show periodicals in an online format. Some contain the entire periodical; others only contain brief comments about the periodical or specific article.

Orientations: Orientation to the library informs students as to the organization and scope of the school library's resources.

Paraphrase: The act or process of restating or rewording.

Podcasts: A digital audio or video file or recording, usually part of a themed series, that can be downloaded from a Web site to a media player or computer.

Readers'/Information Service: This involves extremely delicate forms of assistance. As a school librarian, you are in the position of crossing a very thin line between reference and readers' service, which accounts for your answering such questions as: What is a good book on 9/11? What is the best novel to read?

Ready-Reference: A term used to describe an information service in which librarians provide easy-to-locate facts in response to fairly simple questions. Ready-reference is all about facts.

Reference Interview: To conduct an appropriate and effective reference interview, specialized skills are required. Some of these skills are tangible—can be taught, practiced, and learned. However, some skills are intangible—your individualism or unique personality. Both tangible and intangible skills combine to create purposeful and interesting communications between the school librarian and the student, and hopefully, a successful reference interview.

Reference Process: Fundamentally, it consists of the entire transaction with the student in the course of which the reference work is carried out. Basically, it contains three primary elements: 1) information; 2) student; and 3) answer.

Reference Resource: This can be defined as materials, from book to computer to periodical to photograph, that can be found anywhere in the library or online. A narrow definition restricts the term to sources specifically designed to be consulted for definite items of information rather than to be examined consecutively.

Research Problem-Solving Strategies: Access, evaluation, organization, and use of information are critical to ease the burden of change and to assist humanity in navigating its course toward the future.

Research Process/Information Seeking Process: This model connects information handling and use with subject matter that is essential for learning to occur. This process was developed by Stripling and Pitts.

Resource: Any source or material, regardless of form or location, that provides necessary information.

RSS Feeds: *RSS* stands for Rich Site Summary. RSS feeds keep track of updates on a Web site. RSS feeds are nothing but blogs making a log of a Web site.

Search Engines: A computer program that searches documents, especially on the World Wide Web, for a specified word or words and provides a list of documents in which they are found.

Selection Process: This is the process of deciding what materials to add to the school library media collection. In choosing reference resources, a school librarian plans and carries out certain activities that culminate in selection decisions.

Single Volume Encyclopedia: These encyclopedias meet the needs of students interested in a single fact, place, or phenomenon. They are concise works of information that are excellent for ready-reference factual questions.

***Standards for the 21ˢᵗ-Century Learner*:** This outlines the skills, dispositions, and responsibilities of students to be truly information literate in today's society, including the ability to inquire, think critically, draw conclusions, share information, make informed decisions, and apply knowledge to new situations.

Super3 Information Problem Solving Model: The Super3 Information problem-solving model was adapted from the Big6 to be used with P–2 students. The Super3 uses a simple three-step process to guide young children through the inquiry process.

Thematic Atlases: These emphasize a specific subject or region.

Thesaurus: A specialized dictionary that deals solely with word synonyms and antonyms.

Vendor: A person or agency that sells.

Virtual Reference: The reference process/interview conducted totally online.

Web 2.0: The Internet viewed as a medium in which interactive experience, in the form of blogs, wikis, forums, etc., plays a more important role than simply accessing information.

Webliography: A bibliography that uses only online sources.

Wiktionary: This uses the social media model for developing and maintaining the contents of a "dictionary."

Yearbooks: They present facts and statistics for a single year (primarily the year preceding the publication date).

Works Cited

AASL. *Empowering Learners: Guidelines for School Library Media Programs.* Chicago: AASL, 2009.

AASL. *Standards for the 21st-Century Learner.* Chicago: AASL, 2007.

AASL. *Standards for the 21st-Century Learner in Action.* Chicago: AASL, 2008.

AASL and AECT. *Information Power Building Partnerships for Learning.* Chicago: American Library Association, 1998.

Eisenberg, Michael. "Big6 TIPS: Teaching Information Problem Solving: Information Seeking Strategies." *Emergency Librarian* (1997): 25, 22.

Eisenberg, Michael. "Information Literacy: Essential Skills for the Information Age." *Journal of Library & Information Technology* 28, no. 2 (2008): 39–47.

Katz, William. *Introduction to Reference Work: Information Sources.* 7th ed. New York: McGraw-Hill, 1997.

Katz, William. *Introduction to Reference Work,* vol. 1: *Basic Information Services.* 8th ed. New York: McGraw-Hill, 2002.

Kuhlthau, Carol Collier. "Inside the Search Process: Information Seeking from the User's Perspective." *Journal of the American Society for Information Science* 42, no. 5 (1991): 361–71.

Kuhlthau, Carol Collier. "Learning in Digital Libraries: An Information Search Process Approach." *Library Trends* 45, no. 4 (1997): 708–24.

Levine-Clark, Michael, and Toni M. Carter. *ALA Glossary of Library and Information Science.* 4th ed. Chicago: ALA Editions, 2012.

Loertscher, David, Carol Koechlin, and Sandi Zwann. *The New Learning Commons: Where Learners Win!* 2nd ed. Salt Lake City: Hi Willow Research and Publishing, 2011.

Partnership for 21st Century Skills."21st Century Learning Environments." Retrieved from http://www.21stcenturyskills.org/documents/le_white_paper-1.pdf.

Pitts, Judy. "Six Research Lessons from the Other Side." *The Book Report* 11 (1993): 22–24.

"Presidential Committee on Information Literacy: Final Report," American Library Association, July 24, 2006. http://www.ala.org/acrl/publications/whitepapers/presidential (accessed March 5, 2012). Document ID: 106e5565–9ab9-ad94–8d9f-64962ebcde46

Safford, Barbara Ripp. *Guide to Reference Materials for School Library Media Centers.* 6th ed. Santa Barbara, CA: Libraries Unlimited, 2010.

Scholastic. *School Libraries Work*. 3rd ed. New York: Scholastic Library Publishing, 2008. Retrieved from www.scholastic.com/content/collateral_resources/.../ slw3_2008.pdf.

Strayer, Joseph, ed. *The ALA Glossary of Library and Information Science*. Chicago: American Library Association, 1983.

Todd, Ross. "From Net Surfers to Net Seekers: WWW, Critical Literacies and Learning Outcomes." *Teacher Librarian* 26, no. 2 (1997): 16–21.

Todd, Ross. "WWW, Critical Literacies and Learning Outcomes." *Teacher Librarian* 26, no. 2 (1998): 16.

Whittaker, Kenneth. "Towards a Theory for Reference and Information Services." *Journal of Librarianship* 9 (1977): 49–63.

Woolls, Blanche. *The School Library Media Manager*. 2nd ed. Englewood, CO: Libraries Unlimited, 1999.

Woolls, Blanche. *The School Library Media Manager*, 4th ed. Westport, CT: Libraries Unlimited, 2008.

Index

About the Authors

ANN MARLOW RIEDLING, MEd, MLS, PhD, is associate professor at San Jose State University, San Jose, CA. Her published works are numerous, including 13 textbooks and many scholarly articles and case studies. She graduated from Indiana University with a bachelor's degree, the University of Georgia with master's degrees in education and library and information science, and the University of Louisville with a doctorate in educational administration. Riedling also holds a doctorate in theology and Christian education.

LORETTA SHAKE, EdD, is library media specialist and school technology coordinator for North Oldham Middle School in Goshen, KY. Previously she worked for Jefferson County Public Schools as the computer lab teacher and school technology coordinator at Farnsley Middle School, both in Louisville, KY. Shake received her doctorate from Spalding University in Louisville, KY, and earned bachelor's and master's degrees from the University of Louisville. Her published work includes coauthoring the textbook *Basic Computer Skills*.

CYNTHIA HOUSTON, PhD, is associate professor in the Library Media Education program at Western Kentucky University, Bowling Green, KY. She holds a master's degree in library science from Clarion University and a doctorate in curriculum and instruction from Southern Illinois University–Carbondale. She has been published in a wide range of journals on a variety of topics in library science, including classification, Web 2.0, regional children's literature, and fotonovelas.